GREEK
TRAGEDIES

VOLUME

3

AESCHYLUS

THE EUMENIDES
Translated by Richmond Lattimore

SOPHOCLES

PHILOCTETES
Translated by David Grene

OEDIPUS AT COLONUS
Translated by Robert Fitzgerald

EURIPIDES

THE BACCHAE
Translated by William Arrowsmith

ALCESTIS
Translated by Richmond Lattimore

GREEK TRAGEDIES

Edited by

DAVID GRENE *and* RICHMOND LATTIMORE

VOLUME

3

THE UNIVERSITY OF CHICAGO PRESS

CHICAGO & LONDON

THE UNIVERSITY OF CHICAGO PRESS, CHICAGO 60637

The University of Chicago Press, Ltd., London

International Standard Book Number: 0–226–30777–8
Library of Congress Catalog Card Number: 60–950

NOTE

For this selection from *The Complete Greek Tragedies*, the University of Chicago Press has asked me to write the introductions. Longer and fuller introductions, mostly by the translators themselves, will be found in *The Complete Greek Tragedies*. As befits a limited volume, I have tried to state, very briefly, the essential features of each tragedy here reprinted. The personal views given are, of course, my own, and the translators, other than myself, are not to be held responsible.

R. L.

CONTENTS

THE EUMENIDES

Translated by Richmond Lattimore

INTRODUCTION

The Eumenides was presented in 458 B.C. as the last tragedy in the trilogy called *The Oresteia*. The other plays in the trilogy are *Agamemnon* and *The Libation Bearers*. Each of the three can be studied and interpreted as an independent drama, in isolation from the other two.

When Orestes murdered his mother, he did so by command of Apollo, but even Apollo could not by formal absolution drive away the Furies of the Mother (ultimately canonized as the Eumenides), who pursued the murderer up and down the world. At last the case was brought to Athens and tried by law, before a jury of twelve Athenian citizens, with Athene presiding as judge and Apollo as counsel for the defense. With the count six to six, Athene gave her casting vote for mercy and acquittal, and appeased the Eumenides by establishing them in the place of their subsequent cult, as guardian spirits of Athens.

As a drama of atonement, absolution, and canonization, *The Eumenides* bears some resemblance to Sophocles' *Oedipus at Colonus*. In both cases the hero, morally blameless, is nevertheless contaminated and must be absolved. But Sophocles keeps his supernatural powers in the background. Aeschylus stages his; and his issues are public, not individual, as the story of the Argive House of Atreus in its solution merges into the history of civilization at Athens, which represents in fact the world's progress. Through Athene and the reconciled Eumenides, Aeschylus unmistakably speaks his mind to the Athenians in the stately conclusion of *The Oresteia*.

NOTE

The translation of this play is based on H. W. Smyth's "Loeb Classical Library" text (London and New York: William Heinemann, Ltd., and G. P. Putnam's Sons, 1926). A few deviations from this text occur where the translator has followed the manuscript readings instead of emendations accepted by Smyth.

Various editions of Greek drama divide the lines of lyric passages in various ways, but editors regularly follow the traditional line numbers whether their own line divisions tally with these numbers or not. This accounts for what may appear to be erratic line numbering in this translation, for instance, line 360 and following. The line numbering in this translation is that of Smyth's text.

CHARACTERS

Priestess of Apollo, the Pythia

Apollo

Hermes (silent)

Ghost of Clytaemestra

Orestes

Athene

Chorus of Eumenides (Furies)

Second Chorus; women of Athens

Jurymen, herald, citizens of Athens (all silent parts)

THE EUMENIDES

(Enter, alone, the Pythia.)

Pythia

I give first place of honor in my prayer to her
who of the gods first prophesied, the Earth; and next
to Themis, who succeeded to her mother's place
of prophecy; so runs the legend; and in third
succession, given by free consent, not won by force,   5
another Titan daughter of Earth was seated here.
This was Phoebe. She gave it as a birthday gift
to Phoebus, who is called still after Phoebe's name.
And he, leaving the pond of Delos and the reef,
grounded his ship at the roadstead of Pallas, then   10
made his way to this land and a Parnassian home.
Deep in respect for his degree Hephaestus' sons
conveyed him here, for these are builders of roads, and changed
the wilderness to a land that was no wilderness.
He came so, and the people highly honored him,   15
with Delphus, lord and helmsman of the country. Zeus
made his mind full with godship and prophetic craft
and placed him, fourth in a line of seers, upon this throne.
So, Loxias is the spokesman of his father, Zeus.
These are the gods I set in the proem of my prayer.   20
But Pallas-before-the-temple has her right in all
I say. I worship the nymphs where the Corycian rock
is hollowed inward, haunt of birds and paced by gods.
Bromius, whom I forget not, sways this place. From here
in divine form he led his Bacchanals in arms   25

to hunt down Pentheus like a hare in the deathtrap.
I call upon the springs of Pleistus, on the power
of Poseidon, and on final loftiest Zeus,
then go to sit in prophecy on the throne. May all
grant me that this of all my entrances shall be   30
the best by far. If there are any Hellenes here
let them draw lots, so enter, as the custom is.
My prophecy is only as the god may guide.

(*She enters the temple and almost immediately comes out again.*)

Things terrible to tell and for the eyes to see
terrible drove me out again from Loxias' house   35
so that I have no strength and cannot stand on springing
feet, but run with hands' help and my legs have no speed.
An old woman afraid is nothing: a child, no more.

See, I am on my way to the wreath-hung recess
and on the centrestone I see a man with god's   40
defilement on him postured in the suppliant's seat
with blood dripping from his hands and from a new-drawn
    sword,
holding too a branch that had grown high on an olive
tree, decorously wrapped in a great tuft of wool,
and the fleece shone. So far, at least, I can speak clear.   45

In front of this man slept a startling company
of women lying all upon the chairs. Or not
women, I think I call them rather gorgons, only
not gorgons either, since their shape is not the same.
I saw some creatures painted in a picture once,   50
who tore the food from Phineus, only these had no
wings, that could be seen; they are black and utterly
repulsive, and they snore with breath that drives one back.
From their eyes drips the foul ooze, and their dress is such
as is not right to wear in the presence of the gods'   55
statues, nor even into any human house.
I have never seen the tribe that owns this company
nor know what piece of earth can claim with pride it bore

such brood, and without hurt and tears for labor given.

Now after this the master of the house must take 60
his own measures: Apollo Loxias, who is very strong
and heals by divination; reads portentous signs,
and so clears out the houses others hold as well.

(Exit. The doors of the temple open and show Orestes sur-
rounded by the sleeping Furies, Apollo and
Hermes beside him.)

Apollo

I will not give you up. Through to the end standing
your guardian, whether by your side or far away, 65
I shall not weaken toward your enemies. See now
how I have caught and overpowered these lewd creatures.
The repulsive maidens have been stilled to sleep, those gray
and aged children, they with whom no mortal man,
no god, nor even any beast, will have to do. 70
It was because of evil they were born, because
they hold the evil darkness of the Pit below
Earth, loathed alike by men and by the heavenly gods.
Nevertheless, run from them, never weaken. They
will track you down as you stride on across the long 75
land, and your driven feet forever pound the earth,
on across the main water and the circle-washed
cities. Be herdsman to this hard march. Never fail
until you come at last to Pallas' citadel.
Kneel there, and clasp the ancient idol in your arms, 80
and there we shall find those who will judge this case, and words
to say that will have magic in their figures. Thus
you will be rid of your afflictions, once for all.
For it was I who made you strike your mother down.

Orestes

My lord Apollo, you understand what it means to do 85
no wrong. Learn also what it is not to neglect.
None can mistrust your power to do good, if you will.

Apollo

> Remember: the fear must not give you a beaten heart.
> Hermes, you are my brother from a single sire.
> Look after him, and as you are named the god who guides,   90
> be such in strong fact. He is my suppliant. Shepherd him
> with fortunate escort on his journeys among men.
> The wanderer has rights which Zeus acknowledges.

> > (*Exit Apollo, then Orestes guided by Hermes. Enter the*
> > *ghost of Clytaemestra.*)

Clytaemestra

> You would sleep, then? And what use are you, if you sleep?
> It is because of you I go dishonored thus   95
> among the rest of the dead. Because of those I killed
> my bad name among the perished suffers no eclipse
> but I am driven in disgrace. I say to you
> that I am charged with guilt most grave by these. And yet
> I suffered too, horribly, and from those most dear,   100
> yet none among the powers is angered for my sake
> that I was slaughtered, and by matricidal hands.
> Look at these gashes in my heart, think where they came
> from. Eyes illuminate the sleeping brain,
> but in the daylight man's future cannot be seen.   105
>
> > Yet I have given you much to lap up, outpourings
> without wine, sober propitiations, sacrificed
> in secrecy of night and on a hearth of fire
> for you, at an hour given to no other god.
> Now I watch all these honors trampled into the ground,   110
> and he is out and gone away like any fawn
> so lightly, from the very middle of your nets,
> sprung clear, and laughing merrily at you. Hear me.
> It is my life depends upon this spoken plea.
> Think then, o goddesses beneath the ground. For I,   115
> the dream of Clytaemestra, call upon your name.

> > (*The Furies stir in their sleep and whimper.*)

Clytaemestra

Oh, whimper, then, but your man has got away and gone
far. He has friends to help him, who are not like mine.

(*They whimper again.*)   120

Clytaemestra

Too much sleep and no pity for my plight. I stand,
his mother, here, killed by Orestes. He is gone.

(*They moan in their sleep.*)

Clytaemestra

You moan, you sleep. Get on your feet quickly, will you?
What have you yet got done, except to do evil?   125

(*They moan again.*)

Clytaemestra

Sleep and fatigue, two masterful conspirators,
have dimmed the deadly anger of the mother-snake.

(*The Chorus start violently, then speak in their sleep.*)

Chorus

Get him, get him, get him, get him. Make sure.   130

Clytaemestra

The beast you are after is a dream, but like the hound
whose thought of hunting has no lapse, you bay him on.
What are you about? Up, let not work's weariness
beat you, nor slacken with sleep so you forget my pain.
Scold your own heart and hurt it, as it well deserves,   135
for this is discipline's spur upon her own. Let go
upon this man the stormblasts of your bloodshot breath,
wither him in your wind, after him, hunt him down
once more, and shrivel him in your vitals' heat and flame.

(*The ghost disappears, and the Chorus waken and, as they
waken, speak severally.*)

Chorus

Waken. You are awake, wake her, as I did you.   140
You dream still? On your feet and kick your sleep aside.
Let us see whether this morning-song means vanity.

                                     (Here they begin to howl.)

Sisters, we have had wrong done us.
When I have undergone so much and all in vain.
Suffering, suffering, bitter, oh shame shame,   145
unendurable wrong.
The hunted beast has slipped clean from our nets and gone.
Sleep won me, and I lost my capture.

Shame, son of Zeus! Robber is all you are.
A young god, you have ridden down powers gray with age,   150
taken the suppliant, though a godless man, who hurt
the mother who gave him birth.
Yourself a god, you stole the matricide away.
Where in this act shall any man say there is right?

The accusation came upon me from my dreams,   155
and hit me, as with goad in the mid-grip of his fist
the charioteer strikes,
but deep, beneath lobe and heart.
The executioner's cutting whip is mine to feel   160
and the weight of pain is big, heavy to bear.

Such are the actions of the younger gods. These hold
by unconditional force, beyond all right, a throne
that runs reeking blood,
blood at the feet, blood at the head.
The very stone centre of earth here in our eyes horrible   165
with blood and curse stands plain to see.

Himself divine, he has spoiled his secret shrine's
hearth with the stain, driven and hallooed the action on.   170
He made man's way cross the place of the ways of god
and blighted age-old distributions of power.

He has wounded me, but he shall not get this man away.
Let him hide under the ground, he shall never go free.   175
Cursed suppliant, he shall feel against his head
another murderer rising out of the same seed.

(*Apollo enters again from his sanctuary.*)

Apollo

Get out, I tell you, go and leave this house. Away
in haste, from your presence set the mantic chamber free,   180
else you may feel the flash and bite of a flying snake
launched from the twisted thong of gold that spans my bow
to make you in your pain spew out the black and foaming
blood of men, vomit the clots sucked from their veins.
This house is no right place for such as you to cling   185
upon; but where, by judgment given, heads are lopped
and eyes gouged out, throats cut, and by the spoil of sex
the glory of young boys is defeated, where mutilation
lives, and stoning, and the long moan of tortured men
spiked underneath the spine and stuck on pales. Listen   190
to how the gods spit out the manner of that feast
your loves lean to. The whole cast of your shape is guide
to what you are, the like of whom should hole in the cave
of the blood-reeking lion, not in oracular
interiors, like mine nearby, wipe off your filth.   195
Out then, you flock of goats without a herdsman, since
no god has such affection as to tend this brood.

Chorus

My lord Apollo, it is your turn to listen now.
Your own part in this is more than accessory.
You are the one who did it; all the guilt is yours.   200

Apollo

So? How? Continue speaking, until I understand.

Chorus

You gave this outlander the word to kill his mother.

Apollo

The word to exact price for his father. What of that?

Chorus

You then dared take him in, fresh from his bloodletting.

Apollo

Yes, and I told him to take refuge in this house.   205

Chorus

You are abusive then to those who sped him here?

Apollo

Yes. It was not for you to come near this house;

Chorus

                              and yet
we have our duty. It was to do what we have done.

Apollo

An office? You? Sound forth your glorious privilege.

Chorus

This: to drive matricides out of their houses.   210

Apollo

                                   Then
what if it be the woman and she kills her man?

Chorus

Such murder would not be the shedding of kindred blood.

Apollo

You have made into a thing of no account, no place,
the sworn faith of Zeus and of Hera, lady
of consummations, and Cypris by such argument   215
is thrown away, outlawed, and yet the sweetest things
in man's life come from her, for married love between
man and woman is bigger than oaths, guarded by right
of nature. If when such kill each other you relent
so as not to take vengeance nor eye them in wrath,   220

then I deny your manhunt of Orestes goes
with right. I see that one cause moves you to strong rage
but on the other clearly you are unmoved to act.
Pallas divine shall review the pleadings of this case.

Chorus

Nothing will ever make me let that man go free.   225

Apollo

Keep after him then, and make more trouble for yourselves.

Chorus

Do not try to dock my privilege by argument.

Apollo

I would not take your privilege if you gave it me.

Chorus

No, for you are called great beside the throne of Zeus
already, but the motherblood drives me, and I go   230
to win my right upon this man and hunt him down.

Apollo

But I shall give the suppliant help and rescue, for
if I willingly fail him who turns to me for aid,
his wrath, before gods and men, is a fearful thing.

> (*They go out, separately. The scene is now Athens, on the
> Acropolis before the temple and statue of Athene.
> Orestes enters and takes suppliant posture
> at the feet of the statue.*)

Orestes

My lady Athene, it is at Loxias' behest   235
I come. Then take in of your grace the wanderer
who comes, no suppliant, not unwashed of hand, but one
blunted at last, and worn and battered on the outland
habitations and the beaten ways of men.
Crossing the dry land and the sea alike, keeping   240
the ordinances of Apollo's oracle

I come, goddess, before your statue and your house
to keep watch here and wait the issue of my trial.

(*The Chorus enter severally, looking for Orestes.*)

Chorus

So. Here the man has left a clear trail behind; keep on,   245
keep on, as the unspeaking accuser tells us, by
whose sense, like hounds after a bleeding fawn, we trail
our quarry by the splash and drip of blood. And now
my lungs are blown with abundant and with wearisome
work, mankilling. My range has been the entire extent
of land, and, flown unwinged across the open water,   250
I am here, and give way to no ship in my pursuit.
Our man has gone to cover somewhere in this place.
The welcome smell of human blood has told me so.

Look again, look again,
search everywhere, let   255
not the matricide
steal away and escape.

(*They see Orestes.*)

See there! He clings to defence
again, his arms winding the immortal goddess'
image, so tries to be quit out of our hands.   260
It shall not be. His mother's blood spilled on the ground
can not come back again.
It is all soaked and drained into the ground and gone.

You must give back for her blood from the living man
red blood of your body to suck, and from your own   265
I could feed, with bitter-swallowed drench,
turn your strength limp while yet you live and drag you down
where you must pay for the pain of the murdered mother,
and watch the rest of the mortals stained with violence
against god or guest   270
or hurt parents who were close and dear,
each with the pain upon him that his crime deserves.
Hades is great, Hades calls men to reckoning

there under the ground,
sees all, and cuts it deep in his recording mind.   275

Orestes

I have been beaten and been taught, I understand
the many rules of absolution, where it is right
to speak and where be silent. In this action now
speech has been ordered by my teacher, who is wise.
The stain of blood dulls now and fades upon my hand.   280
My blot of matricide is being washed away.
When it was fresh still, at the hearth of the god, Phoebus,
this was absolved and driven out by sacrifice
of swine, and the list were long if I went back to tell
of all I met who were not hurt by being with me.   285
Time in his aging overtakes all things alike.
Now it is from pure mouth and with good auspices
I call upon Athene, queen of this land, to come
and rescue me. She, without work of her spear, shall win
myself and all my land and all the Argive host   290
to stand her staunch companion for the rest of time.
Whether now ranging somewhere in the Libyan land
beside her father's crossing and by Triton's run
of waters she sets upright or enshrouded foot
rescuing there her friends, or on the Phlegraean flat   295
like some bold man of armies sweeps with eyes the scene,
let her come! She is a god and hears me far away.
So may she set me free from what is at my back.

Chorus

Neither Apollo nor Athene's strength must win
you free, save you from going down forgotten, without   300
knowing where joy lies anywhere inside your heart,
blood drained, chewed dry by the powers of death, a wraith, a
    shell.
You will not speak to answer, spew my challenge away?
You are consecrate to me and fattened for my feast,

and you shall feed me while you live, not cut down first   305
at the altar. Hear the spell I sing to bind you in.

Come then, link we our choral. Ours
to show forth the power
and terror of our music, declare
our rights of office, how we conspire   310
to steer men's lives.
We hold we are straight and just. If a man
can spread his hands and show they are clean,
no wrath of ours shall lurk for him.
Unscathed he walks through his life time.   315
But one like this man before us, with stained
hidden hands, and the guilt upon him,
shall find us beside him, as witnesses
of the truth, and we show clear in the end
to avenge the blood of the murdered.   320

Mother, o my mother night, who gave me
birth, to be a vengeance on the seeing
and the blind, hear me. For Leto's
youngling takes my right away,
stealing from my clutch the prey   325
that crouches, whose blood would wipe
at last the motherblood away.

Over the beast doomed to the fire
this is the chant, scatter of wits,
frenzy and fear, hurting the heart,   330
song of the Furies
binding brain and blighting blood
in its stringless melody.

This the purpose that the all-involving
destiny spun, to be ours and to be shaken   335
never: when mortals assume outrage
of own hand in violence,
these we dog, till one goes

under earth. Nor does death
set them altogether free.   340

Over the beast doomed to the fire
this is the chant, scatter of wits,
frenzy and fear, hurting the heart,
song of the Furies
binding brain and blighting blood   345
in its stringless melody.

When we were born such lots were assigned for our keeping.
So the immortals must hold hands off, nor is there   350
one who shall sit at our feasting.
For sheer white robes I have no right and no portion.

I have chosen overthrow
of houses, where the Battlegod   355
grown within strikes near and dear
down. So we swoop upon this man
here. He is strong, but we wear him down
for the blood that is still wet on him.

Here we stand in our haste to wrench from all others   360
these devisings, make the gods clear of our counsels
so that even appeal comes
not to them, since Zeus has ruled our blood dripping company   365
outcast, nor will deal with us.

I have chosen overthrow
of houses, where the Battlegod
grown within strikes near and dear
down. So we swoop upon this man
here. He is strong, but we wear him down
for the blood that is still wet on him.

Men's illusions in their pride under the sky melt
down, and are diminished into the ground, gone
before the onset of our black robes, pulsing   370
of our vindictive feet against them.

For with a long leap from high
above and dead drop of weight
I bring foot's force crashing down
to cut the legs from under even   375
the runner, and spill him to ruin.

He falls, and does not know in the daze of his folly.
Such in the dark of man is the mist of infection
that hovers, and moaning rumor tells how his house lies
under fog that glooms above.   380

For with a long leap from high
above, and dead drop of weight,
I bring foot's force crashing down
to cut the legs from under even
the runner, and spill him to ruin.

All holds. For we are strong and skilled;
we have authority; we hold
memory of evil; we are stern
nor can men's pleadings bend us. We
drive through our duties, spurned, outcast   385
from gods, driven apart to stand in light
not of the sun. So sheer with rock are ways
for those who see, as upon those whose eyes are lost.

Is there a man who does not fear
this, does not shrink to hear   390
how my place has been ordained,
granted and given by destiny
and god, absolute? Privilege
primeval yet is mine, nor am I without place
though it be underneath the ground   395
and in no sunlight and in gloom that I must stand.

                          (Athene enters, in full armor.)

Athene

From far away I heard the outcry of your call.
It was beside Scamandrus. I was taking seisin
of land, for there the Achaean lords of war and first

fighters gave me large portion of all their spears   400
had won, the land root and stock to be mine for all
eternity, for the sons of Theseus a choice gift.
From there, sped on my weariless feet, I came, wingless
but in the rush and speed of the aegis fold. And now
I see upon this land a novel company   405
which, though it brings no terror to my eyes, brings still
wonder. Who are you? I address you all alike,
both you, the stranger kneeling at my image here,
and you, who are like no seed ever begotten, not   410
seen ever by the gods as goddesses, nor yet
stamped in the likenesses of any human form.
But no. This is the place of the just. Its rights forbid
even the innocent to speak evil of his mates.

Chorus

Daughter of Zeus, you shall hear all compressed to brief   415
measure. We are the gloomy children of the night.
Curses they call us in our homes beneath the ground.

Athene

I know your race, then, and the names by which you are called.

Chorus

You shall be told of our position presently.

Athene

I can know that, if one will give me a clear account.   420

Chorus

We drive from home those who have shed the blood of men.

Athene

Where is the place, then, where the killer's flight shall end?

Chorus

A place where happiness is nevermore allowed.

Athene

Is he one? Do you blast him to this kind of flight?

Chorus

 Yes. He murdered his mother by deliberate choice.   425

Athene

 By random force, or was it fear of someone's wrath?

Chorus

 Where is the spur to justify man's matricide?

Athene

 Here are two sides, and only half the argument.

Chorus

 He is unwilling to give or to accept an oath.

Athene

 You wish to be called righteous rather than act right.   430

Chorus

 No. How so? Out of the riches of your wit, explain.

Athene

 I say, wrong must not win by technicalities.

Chorus

 Examine him then yourself. Decide it, and be fair.

Athene

 You would turn over authority in this case to me?

Chorus

 By all means. Your father's degree, and yours, deserve as much.   435

Athene

 Your turn, stranger. What will you say in answer? Speak,
tell me your country and your birth, what has befallen
you, then defend yourself against the anger of these;
if it was confidence in the right that made you sit
to keep this image near my hearth, a supplicant   440
in the tradition of Ixion, sacrosanct.
Give me an answer which is plain to understand.

Orestes

    Lady Athene, first I will take the difficult thought
    away that lies in these last words you spoke. I am
    no supplicant, nor was it because I had a stain   445
    upon my hand that I sat at your image. I
    will give you a strong proof that what I say is true.
    It is the law that the man of the bloody hand must speak
    no word until, by action of one who can cleanse,
    blood from a young victim has washed his blood away.   450
    Long since, at the homes of others, I have been absolved
    thus, both by running waters and by victims slain.

    I count this scruple now out of the way. Learn next
    with no delay where I am from. I am of Argos
    and it is to my honor that you ask the name   455
    of my father, Agamemnon, lord of seafarers,
    and your companion when you made the Trojan city
    of Ilium no city any more. He died
    without honor when he came home. It was my mother
    of the dark heart, who entangled him in subtle gyves   460
    and cut him down. The bath is witness to his death.
    I was an exile in the time before this. I came back
    and killed the woman who gave me birth. I plead guilty.
    My father was dear, and this was vengeance for his blood.
    Apollo shares responsibility for this.   465
    He counterspurred my heart and told me of pains to come
    if I should fail to act against the guilty ones.
    This is my case. Decide if it be right or wrong.
    I am in your hands. Where my fate falls, I shall accept.

Athene

    The matter is too big for any mortal man   470
    who thinks he can judge it. Even I have not the right
    to analyse cases of murder where wrath's edge
    is sharp, and all the more since you have come, and clung
    a clean and innocent supplicant, against my doors.
    You bring no harm to my city. I respect your rights.   475

Yet these, too, have their work. We cannot brush them aside,
and if this action so runs that they fail to win,
the venom of their resolution will return
to infect the soil, and sicken all my land to death.
Here is dilemma. Whether I let them stay or drive   480
them off, it is a hard course and will hurt. Then, since
the burden of the case is here, and rests on me,
I shall select judges of manslaughter, and swear
them in, establish a court into all time to come.

Litigants, call your witnesses, have ready your proofs   485
as evidence under bond to keep this case secure.
I will pick the finest of my citizens, and come
back. They shall swear to make no judgment that is not
just, and make clear where in this action the truth lies.

                                              (Exit.)

Chorus

Here is overthrow of all   490
the young laws, if the claim
of this matricide shall stand
good, his crime be sustained.
Should this be, every man will find a way
to act at his own caprice;   495
over and over again in time
to come, parents shall await
the deathstroke at their children's hands.

We are the Angry Ones. But we
shall watch no more over works   500
of men, and so act. We shall
let loose indiscriminate death.
Man shall learn from man's lot, forejudge
the evils of his neighbor's case,
see respite and windfall in storm:
pathetic prophet who consoles   505
with strengthless cures, in vain.

Nevermore let one who feels
the stroke of accident, uplift
his voice and make outcry, thus: 510
"Oh Justice!
Throned powers of the Furies, help!"
Such might be the pitiful cry
of some father, of the stricken
mother, their appeal. Now   515
the House of Justice has collapsed.

There are times when fear is good.
It must keep its watchful place
at the heart's controls. There is
advantage   520
in the wisdom won from pain.
Should the city, should the man
rear a heart that nowhere goes
in fear, how shall such a one
any more respect the right?   525

Refuse the life of anarchy;
refuse the life devoted to
one master.
The in-between has the power
by God's grant always, though   530
his ordinances vary.
I will speak in defence
of reason: for the very child
of vanity is violence;
but out of health   535
in the heart issues the beloved
and the longed-for, prosperity.

All for all I say to you:
bow before the altar of right.
You shall not   540
eye advantage, and heel
it over with foot of force.

Vengeance will be upon you.
The all is bigger than you.
Let man see this and take   545
care, to mother and father,
and to the guest
in the gates welcomed, give all rights
that befall their position.

The man who does right, free-willed, without constraint   550
shall not lose happiness
nor be wiped out with all his generation.
But the transgressor, I tell you, the bold man
who brings in confusion of goods unrightly won,
at long last and perforce, when ship toils   555
under tempest must strike his sail
in the wreck of his rigging.

He calls on those who hear not, caught inside
the hard wrestle of water.
The spirit laughs at the hot hearted man,   560
the man who said "never to me," watches him
pinned in distress, unable to run free of the crests.
He had good luck in his life. Now
he smashes it on the reef of Right
and drowns, unwept and forgotten.   565

*(Athene re-enters, guiding twelve citizens chosen as jurors
and attended by a herald. Other citizens follow.)*

Athene

Herald, make proclamation and hold in the host
assembled. Let the stabbing voice of the Etruscan
trumpet, blown to the full with mortal wind, crash out
its high call to all the assembled populace
For in the filling of this senatorial ground   570
it is best for all the city to be silent and learn
the measures I have laid down into the rest of time.
So too these litigants, that their case be fairly tried.

(Trumpet call. All take their places. Enter Apollo.)

Chorus

    My lord Apollo, rule within your own domain.

    What in this matter has to do with you? Declare.   575

Apollo

    I come to testify. This man, by observed law,

    came to me as suppliant, took his place by hearth and hall,

    and it was I who cleaned him of the stain of blood.

    I have also come to help him win his case. I bear

    responsibility for his mother's murder.

                            (To Athene.)

                           You   580

    who know the rules, initiate the trial. Preside.

Athene (to the Furies)

    I declare the trial opened. Yours is the first word.

    For it must justly be the pursuer who speaks first

    and opens the case, and makes plain what the action is.

Chorus

    We are many, but we shall cut it short. You, then,   585

    word against word answer our charges one by one.

    Say first, did you kill your mother or did you not?

Orestes

    Yes, I killed her. There shall be no denial of that.

Chorus

    There are three falls in the match and one has gone to us.

Orestes

    So you say. But you have not even thrown your man.   590

Chorus

    So. Then how did you kill her? You are bound to say.

Orestes

    I do. With drawn sword in my hand I cut her throat.

Chorus

    By whose persuasion and advice did you do this?

Orestes

By order of this god, here. So he testifies.

Chorus

The Prophet guided you into this matricide? 595

Orestes

Yes. I have never complained of this. I do not now.

Chorus

When sentence seizes you, you will talk a different way.

Orestes

I have no fear. My father will aid me from the grave.

Chorus

Kill your mother, then put trust in a corpse! Trust on.

Orestes

Yes. She was dirtied twice over with disgrace. 600

Chorus

Tell me how, and explain it to the judges here.

Orestes

She murdered her husband, and thereby my father too.

Chorus

Of this stain, death has set her free. But you still live.

Orestes

When she lived, why did you not descend and drive her out?

Chorus

The man she killed was not of blood congenital. 605

Orestes

But am I then involved with my mother by blood-bond?

Chorus

Murderer, yes. How else could she have nursed you beneath her heart? Do you forswear your mother's intimate blood?

Orestes

    Yours to bear witness now, Apollo, and expound
    the case for me, if I was right to cut her down.   610
    I will not deny I did this thing, because I did
    do it. But was the bloodshed right or not? Decide
    and answer. As you answer, I shall state my case.

Apollo

    To you, established by Athene in your power,
    I shall speak justly. I am a prophet, I shall not   615
    lie. Never, for man, woman, nor city, from my throne
    of prophecy have I spoken a word, except
    that which Zeus, father of Olympians, might command.
    This is justice. Recognize then how great its strength.
    I tell you, follow our father's will. For not even   620
    the oath that binds you is more strong than Zeus is strong.

Chorus

    Then Zeus, as you say, authorized the oracle
    to this Orestes, stating he could wreak the death
    of his father on his mother, and it would have no force?

Apollo

    It is not the same thing for a man of blood to die   625
    honored with the king's staff given by the hand of god,
    and that by means of a woman, not with the far cast
    of fierce arrows, as an Amazon might have done,
    but in a way that you shall hear, o Pallas and you
    who sit in state to judge this action by your vote.   630

    He had come home from his campaigning. He had done
    better than worse, in the eyes of a fair judge. She lay
    in wait for him. It was the bath. When he was at
    its edge, she hooded the robe on him, and in the blind
    and complex toils tangled her man, and chopped him down.   635

    There is the story of the death of a great man,
    solemn in all men's sight, lord of the host of ships.

I have called the woman what she was, so that the people
whose duty it is to try this case may be inflamed.

Chorus

Zeus, by your story, gives first place to the father's death.   640
Yet Zeus himself shackled elder Cronus, his own
father. Is this not contradiction? I testify,
judges, that this is being said in your hearing.

Apollo

You foul animals, from whom the gods turn in disgust,
Zeus could undo shackles, such hurt can be made good,   645
and there is every kind of way to get out. But once
the dust has drained down all a man's blood, once the man
has died, there is no raising of him up again.
This is a thing for which my father never made
curative spells. All other states, without effort   650
of hard breath, he can completely rearrange.

Chorus

See what it means to force acquittal of this man.
He has spilled his mother's blood upon the ground. Shall he
then be at home in Argos in his father's house?
What altars of the community shall he use? Is there   655
a brotherhood's lustration that will let him in?

Apollo

I will tell you, and I will answer correctly. Watch.
The mother is no parent of that which is called
her child, but only nurse of the new-planted seed
that grows. The parent is he who mounts. A stranger she   660
preserves a stranger's seed, if no god interfere.
I will show you proof of what I have explained. There can
be a father without any mother. There she stands,
the living witness, daughter of Olympian Zeus,
she who was never fostered in the dark of the womb   665
yet such a child as no goddess could bring to birth.
In all else, Pallas, as I best may understand,

I shall make great your city and its populace.
So I have brought this man to sit beside the hearth
of your house, to be your true friend for the rest of time,   670
so you shall win him, goddess, to fight by your side,
and among men to come this shall stand a strong bond
that his and your own people's children shall be friends.

Athene

Shall I assume that enough has now been said, and tell
the judges to render what they believe a true verdict?   675

Chorus

Every arrow we had has been shot now. We wait
on their decision, to see how the case has gone.

Athene

So then. How shall I act correctly in your eyes?

Apollo

You have heard what you have heard, and as you cast your votes,
good friends, respect in your hearts the oath that you have sworn.   680

Athene

If it please you, men of Attica, hear my decree
now, on this first case of bloodletting I have judged.
For Aegeus' population, this forevermore
shall be the ground where justices deliberate.
Here is the Hill of Ares, here the Amazons   685
encamped and built their shelters when they came in arms
for spite of Theseus, here they piled their rival towers
to rise, new city, and dare his city long ago,
and slew their beasts for Ares. So this rock is named
from then the Hill of Ares. Here the reverence   690
of citizens, their fear and kindred do-no-wrong
shall hold by day and in the blessing of night alike
all while the people do not muddy their own laws
with foul infusions. But if bright water you stain
with mud, you nevermore will find it fit to drink.   695

No anarchy, no rule of a single master. Thus
I advise my citizens to govern and to grace,
and not to cast fear utterly from your city. What
man who fears nothing at all is ever righteous? Such
be your just terrors, and you may deserve and have   700
salvation for your citadel, your land's defence,
such as is nowhere else found among men, neither
among the Scythians, nor the land that Pelops held.
I establish this tribunal. It shall be untouched
by money-making, grave but quick to wrath, watchful   705
to protect those who sleep, a sentry on the land.

These words I have unreeled are for my citizens,
advice into the future. All must stand upright
now, take each man his ballot in his hand, think on
his oath, and make his judgment. For my word is said.   710

Chorus

I give you counsel by no means to disregard
this company. We can be a weight to crush your land.

Apollo

I speak too. I command you to fear, and not
make void the yield of oracles from Zeus and me.

Chorus

You honor bloody actions where you have no right.   715
The oracles you give shall be no longer clean.

Apollo

My father's purposes are twisted then. For he
was appealed to by Ixion, the first murderer.

Chorus

Talk! But for my part, if I do not win the case,
I shall come back to this land and it will feel my weight.   720

Apollo

Neither among the elder nor the younger gods
have you consideration. I shall win this suit.

Chorus

> Such was your action in the house of Pheres. Then
> you beguiled the Fates to let mortals go free from death.

Apollo

> Is it not right to do well by the man who shows   725
> you worship, and above all when he stands in need?

Chorus

> You won the ancient goddesses over with wine
> and so destroyed the orders of an elder time.

Apollo

> You shall not win the issue of this suit, but shall
> be made to void your poison to no enemy's hurt.   730

Chorus

> Since you, a young god, would ride down my elder age,
> I must stay here and listen to how the trial goes,
> being yet uncertain to loose my anger on the state.

Athene

> It is my task to render final judgment here.
> This is a ballot for Orestes I shall cast.   735
> There is no mother anywhere who gave me birth,
> and, but for marriage, I am always for the male
> with all my heart, and strongly on my father's side.
> So, in a case where the wife has killed her husband, lord
> of the house, her death shall not mean most to me. And if   740
> the other votes are even, then Orestes wins.
> You of the jurymen who have this duty assigned,
> shake out the ballots from the vessels, with all speed.

Orestes

> Phoebus Apollo, what will the decision be?

Chorus

> Darkness of night, our mother, are you here to watch?   745

Orestes

This is the end for me. The noose, or else the light.

Chorus

Here our destruction, or our high duties confirmed.

Apollo

Shake out the votes accurately, Athenian friends.
Be careful as you pick them up. Make no mistake.
In the lapse of judgment great disaster comes. The cast   750
of a single ballot has restored a house entire.

Athene

The man before us has escaped the charge of blood.
The ballots are in equal number for each side.

Orestes

Pallas Athene, you have kept my house alive.
When I had lost the land of my fathers you gave me   755
a place to live. Among the Hellenes they shall say:
"A man of Argos lives again in the estates
of his father, all by grace of Pallas Athene, and
Apollo, and with them the all-ordaining god
the Savior"—who remembers my father's death, who looked   760
upon my mother's advocates, and rescues me.
I shall go home now, but before I go I swear
to this your country and to this your multitude
of people into all the bigness of time to be,
that never man who holds the helm of my state shall come   765
against your country in the ordered strength of spears,
but though I lie then in my grave, I still shall wreak
helpless bad luck and misadventure upon all
who stride across the oath that I have sworn: their ways
disconsolate make, their crossings full of evil   770
augury, so they shall be sorry that they moved.
But while they keep the upright way, and hold in high
regard the city of Pallas, and align their spears
to fight beside her, I shall be their gracious spirit.

And so farewell, you and your city's populace.   775
May you outwrestle and overthrow all those who come
against you, to your safety and your spears' success.

(*Exit. Exit also Apollo.*)

Chorus

Gods of the younger generation, you have ridden down
the laws of the elder time, torn them out of my hands.
I, disinherited, suffering, heavy with anger   780
shall let loose on the land
the vindictive poison
dripping deadly out of my heart upon the ground;
this from itself shall breed
cancer, the leafless, the barren   785
to strike, for the right, their low lands
and drag its smear of mortal infection on the ground.
What shall I do? Afflicted
I am mocked by these people.
I have borne what can not   790
be borne. Great the sorrows and the dishonor upon
the sad daughters of night.

Athene

Listen to me. I would not have you be so grieved.
For you have not been beaten. This was the result   795
of a fair ballot which was even. You were not
dishonored, but the luminous evidence of Zeus
was there, and he who spoke the oracle was he
who ordered Orestes so to act and not be hurt.
Do not be angry any longer with this land   800
nor bring the bulk of your hatred down on it, do not
render it barren of fruit, nor spill the dripping rain
of death in fierce and jagged lines to eat the seeds.
In complete honesty I promise you a place
of your own, deep hidden under ground that is yours by right   805
where you shall sit on shining chairs beside the hearth
to accept devotions offered by your citizens.

Chorus

> Gods of the younger generation, you have ridden down
> the laws of the elder time, torn them out of my hands.
> I, disinherited, suffering, heavy with anger   810
> shall let loose on the land
> the vindictive poison
> dripping deadly out of my heart upon the ground;
> this from itself shall breed
> cancer, the leafless, the barren   815
> to strike, for the right, their low lands
> and drag its smear of mortal infection on the ground.
> What shall I do? Afflicted
> I am mocked by these people.
> I have borne what can not   820
> be borne. Great the sorrow and the dishonor upon
> the sad daughters of night.

Athene

> No, not dishonored. You are goddesses. Do not
> in too much anger make this place of mortal men
> uninhabitable. I have Zeus behind me. Do   825
> we need to speak of that? I am the only god
> who know the keys to where his thunderbolts are locked.
> We do not need such, do we? Be reasonable
> and do not from a reckless mouth cast on the land   830
> spells that will ruin every thing which might bear fruit.
> No. Put to sleep the bitter strength in the black wave
> and live with me and share my pride of worship. Here
> is a big land, and from it you shall win first fruits
> in offerings for children and the marriage rite   835
> for always. Then you will say my argument was good.

Chorus

> That they could treat me so!
> I, the mind of the past, to be driven under the ground
> out cast, like dirt!
> The wind I breathe is fury and utter hate.   840

Earth, ah, earth
what is this agony that crawls under my ribs?
Night, hear me, o Night,
mother. They have wiped me out   845
and the hard hands of the gods
and their treacheries have taken my old rights away.

Athene

I will bear your angers. You are elder born than I
and in that you are wiser far than I. Yet still
Zeus gave me too intelligence not to be despised.   850
If you go away into some land of foreigners,
I warn you, you will come to love this country. Time
in his forward flood shall ever grow more dignified
for the people of this city. And you, in your place
of eminence beside Erechtheus in his house   855
shall win from female and from male processionals
more than all lands of men beside could ever give.
Only in this place that I haunt do not inflict
your bloody stimulus to twist the inward hearts
of young men, raging in a fury not of wine,   860
nor, as if plucking the heart from fighting cocks,
engraft among my citizens that spirit of war
that turns their battle fury inward on themselves.
No, let our wars range outward hard against the man
who has fallen horribly in love with high renown.   865
No true fighter I call the bird that fights at home.
Such life I offer you, and it is yours to take.
Do good, receive good, and be honored as the good
are honored. Share our country, the beloved of god.

Chorus

That they could treat me so!   870
I, the mind of the past, to be driven under the ground
out cast, like dirt!
The wind I breathe is fury and utter hate.
Earth, ah, earth

what is this agony that crawls under my ribs?   875
Night, hear me, o Night,
mother. They have wiped me out
and the hard hands of the gods
and their treacheries have taken my old rights away.   880

Athene

I will not weary of telling you all the good things
I offer, so that you can never say that you,
an elder god, were driven unfriended from the land
by me in my youth, and by my mortal citizens.
But if you hold Persuasion has her sacred place   885
of worship, in the sweet beguilement of my voice,
then you might stay with us. But if you wish to stay
then it would not be justice to inflict your rage
upon this city, your resentment or bad luck
to armies. Yours the baron's portion in this land   890
if you will, in all justice, with full privilege.

Chorus

Lady Athene, what is this place you say is mine?

Athene

A place free of all grief and pain. Take it for yours.

Chorus

If I do take it, shall I have some definite powers?

Athene

No household shall be prosperous without your will.   895

Chorus

You will do this? You will really let me be so strong?

Athene

So we shall straighten the lives of all who worship us.

Chorus

You guarantee such honor for the rest of time?

Athene

I have no need to promise what I can not do.

Chorus

I think you will have your way with me. My hate is going.   900

Athene

Stay here, then. You will win the hearts of others, too.

Chorus

I will put a spell upon the land. What shall it be?

Athene

Something that has no traffic with evil success.
Let it come out of the ground, out of the sea's water,
and from the high air make the waft of gentle gales   905
wash over the country in full sunlight, and the seed
and stream of the soil's yield and of the grazing beasts
be strong and never fail our people as time goes,
and make the human seed be kept alive. Make more
the issue of those who worship more your ways, for as   910
the gardener works in love, so love I best of all
the unblighted generation of these upright men.
All such is yours for granting. In the speech and show
and pride of battle, I myself shall not endure
this city's eclipse in the estimation of mankind.   915

Chorus

I accept this home at Athene's side.
I shall not forget the cause
of this city, which Zeus all powerful and Ares
rule, stronghold of divinities,
glory of Hellene gods, their guarded altar.   920
So with forecast of good
I speak this prayer for them
that the sun's bright magnificence shall break out wave
on wave of all the happiness   925
life can give, across their land

Athene

> Here are my actions. In all good will
> toward these citizens I establish in power
> spirits who are large, difficult to soften.
> To them is given the handling entire   930
> of men's lives. That man
> who has not felt the weight of their hands
> takes the strokes of life, knows not whence, not why,
> for crimes wreaked in past generations
> drag him before these powers. Loud his voice   935
> but the silent doom
> hates hard, and breaks him to dust.

Chorus

> Let there blow no wind that wrecks the trees.
> I pronounce words of grace.
> Nor blaze of heat blind the blossoms of grown plants, nor   940
> cross the circles of its right
> place. Let no barren deadly sickness creep and kill.
> Flocks fatten. Earth be kind
> to them, with double fold of fruit   945
> in time appointed for its yielding. Secret child
> of earth, her hidden wealth, bestow
> blessing and surprise of gods.

Athene

> Strong guard of our city, hear you these
> and what they portend? Fury is a high queen   950
> of strength even among the immortal gods
> and the undergods, and for humankind
> their work is accomplished, absolute, clear:
> for some, singing; for some, life dimmed
> in tears; theirs the disposition.   955

Chorus

> Death of manhood cut down
> before its prime I forbid:

girls' grace and glory find
men to live life with them.
Grant, you who have the power.   960
And o, steering spirits of law,
goddesses of destiny,
sisters from my mother, hear;
in all houses implicate,
in all time heavy of hand   965
on whom your just arrest befalls,
august among goddesses, bestow.

Athene

It is my glory to hear how these
generosities
are given my land. I admire the eyes   970
of Persuasion, who guided the speech of my mouth
toward these, when they were reluctant and wild.
Zeus, who guides men's speech in councils, was too
strong; and my ambition
for good wins out in the whole issue.   975

Chorus

This my prayer: Civil War
fattening on men's ruin shall
not thunder in our city. Let
not the dry dust that drinks
the black blood of citizens   980
through passion for revenge
and bloodshed for bloodshed
be given our state to prey upon.
Let them render grace for grace.
Let love be their common will;   985
let them hate with single heart.
Much wrong in the world thereby is healed.

Athene

Are they taking thought to discover that road
where speech goes straight?

In the terror upon the faces of these   990
I see great good for our citizens.
While with good will you hold in high honor
these spirits, their will shall be good, as you steer
your city, your land
on an upright course clear through to the end.   995

Chorus

Farewell, farewell. High destiny shall be yours
by right. Farewell, citizens
seated near the throne of Zeus,
beloved by the maiden he loves,
civilized as years go by,   1000
sheltered under Athene's wings,
grand even in her father's sight.

Athene

Goddesses, farewell. Mine to lead, as these
attend us, to where
by the sacred light new chambers are given.   1005
Go then. Sped by majestic sacrifice
from these, plunge beneath the ground. There hold
off what might hurt the land; pour in
the city's advantage, success in the end.
You, children of Cranaus, you who keep   1010
the citadel, guide these guests of the state.
For good things given,
your hearts' desire be for good to return.

Chorus

Farewell and again farewell, words spoken twice over,
all who by this citadel,   1015
mortal men, spirits divine,
hold the city of Pallas, grace
this my guestship in your land.
Life will give you no regrets.   1020

Athene

    Well said. I assent to all the burden of your prayers,
    and by the light of flaring torches now attend
    your passage to the deep and subterranean hold,
    as by us walk those women whose high privilege
    it is to guard my image. Flower of all the land   1025
    of Theseus, let them issue now, grave companies,
    maidens, wives, elder women, in processional.
    In the investiture of purple stained robes
    dignify them, and let the torchlight go before
    so that the kindly company of these within   1030
    our ground may shine in the future of strong men to come.

Chorus (by the women who have been forming for processional)

    Home, home, o high, o aspiring .
    Daughters of Night, aged children, in blithe processional.
    Bless them, all here, with silence.   1035

    In the primeval dark of earth-hollows
    held in high veneration with rights sacrificial
    bless them, all people, with silence.

    Gracious be, wish what the land wishes,   1040
    follow, grave goddesses, flushed in the flamesprung
    torchlight gay on your journey.
    Singing all follow our footsteps.

    There shall be peace forever between these people
    of Pallas and their guests. Zeus the all seeing   1045
    met with Destiny to confirm it.
    Singing all follow our footsteps.

              (Exeunt omnes, in procession.)

PHILOCTETES

Translated by David Grene

INTRODUCTION

Philoctetes was produced in 409 B.C., when Sophocles was nearly eighty, and won first prize.

Philoctetes was the lawful master of the great bow of Heracles. He joined the Achaean expedition against Troy but, in guiding his mates to a place of sacrifice, he was bitten in the foot by a snake, and the wound would not heal. Because of the stench of the festering sore and the man's inauspicious cries, he was marooned on Lemnos. But after the death of Achilles, the Greeks found from prophecies that they could not take Troy without Philoctetes and his bow, and had to send an embassy to beg or beguile him to come back. Restored and healed at last, he played the leading part in the final battles at Troy. The story is told in the epic continuations of Homer, barely noticed, though obviously known, by Homer himself. It is an excellent theme for tragedy, being an example of a plot fully tragic in the Greek, though perhaps not in the modern, sense, which yet has a necessarily happy ending. Many plays called *Philoctetes* are recorded, but all except the one by Sophocles are lost. Aeschylus produced one, of unknown date, and so did Euripides, along with *Medea* in 431 B.C.

The circumstances of the wound and the plight of Philoctetes, the identity of the hero or heroes assigned to reclaim him, the means used—these vary in the tradition. Here, to Odysseus, the intelligent, persistent, ruthless spirit of the Greek war against Troy, Sophocles has added as collaborator the young Neoptolemus, son of Achilles and pre-eminent fighting man, who, schooled by Odysseus, wins the bow from Philoctetes. But he acts against his nature in so doing. Caught between military duty and his personal integrity, he must, as a Sophoclean hero, follow the dictates of the latter. At the end, he is ready to give up his career of glory and the cause of the Trojan War, and only the command of the deified Heracles saves the situation.

Philoctetes is a drama of the adventures of characters, reduced to its simplest terms. All three main persons are drawn with convincing care. The chorus is minimal, the lyrics reduced in scope. There is almost no decoration. This comes close to being prose drama, in which the·poetry comes unobtrusively, chiefly from Philoctetes' deep love for inanimate or inhuman things—his bow, his wilderness household, and the spirits of the wild place which would have destroyed him but which he has mastered in his lonely struggle for survival.

CHARACTERS

Odysseus

Chorus of Sailors under the Command of Neoptolemus

The Spy Disguised as a Trader

Neoptolemus, Prince of Scyrus and Son of Achilles

Philoctetes

Heracles

PHILOCTETES

SCENE: *A lonely spot on the island of Lemnos. Enter Odysseus and Neoptolemus.*

Odysseus
  This is it; this Lemnos and its beach
  down to the sea that quite surrounds it; desolate,
  no one sets foot on it; there are no houses.
  This is where I marooned him long ago,
  the son of Poias, the Melian, his foot
  diseased and eaten away with running ulcers.

  Son of our greatest hero,
  son of Achilles, Neoptolemus,
  I tell you I had orders for what I did:
  my masters, the princes, bade me do it.

  We had no peace with him: at the holy festivals,
  we dared not touch the wine and meat; he screamed
  and groaned so, and those terrible cries of his
  brought ill luck on our celebrations; all
  the camp was haunted by him.   10

  Now is no time to talk to you of this,
  now is no time for long speeches.
  I am afraid that he may hear of my coming
  and ruin all my plans to take him.

  It is you who must help me with the rest. Look about
  and see where there might be a cave with two mouths.
  There are two niches to rest in, one in the sun
  when it is cold, the other a tunneled passage
  through which the breezes blow in summertime.

A man can sleep there and be cool. To the left,
a little, you may see a spring to drink at—
if it is still unchoked—go this way quietly,
see if he's there or somewhere else and signal.
Then I can tell you the rest. Listen:
I shall tell you. We will both do this thing.

Neoptolemus
What you speak of is near at hand, Odysseus.
I think I see such a cave.

Odysseus
Above or below? I cannot see it myself.

Neoptolemus
Above here, and no trace of a footpath.

Odysseus
See if he is housed within, asleep.

Neoptolemus
I see an empty hut, with no one there.

Odysseus
And nothing to keep house with?

Neoptolemus
A pallet bed, stuffed with leaves, to sleep on, for someone.

Odysseus
And nothing else? Nothing inside the house?

Neoptolemus
A cup, made of a single block, a poor
workman's contrivance. And some kindling, too.

Odysseus
It is his treasure house that you describe.

Neoptolemus
And look, some rags are drying in the sun
full of the oozing matter from a sore.

Odysseus

    Yes, certainly he lives here, even now   40
    is somewhere not far off. He cannot go far,
    sick as he is, lame cripple for so long.
    It's likely he has gone to search for food
    or somewhere that he knows there is a herb
    to ease his pain. Send your man here to watch,
    that he may not come upon me without warning.
    For he would rather take me than all the Greeks.

Neoptolemus

    Very well, then, the path will be watched.
    Go on with your story; tell me what you want.

Odysseus

    Son of Achilles,   50
    our coming here has a purpose; to it be loyal
    with more than with your body. If you should hear
    some strange new thing, unlike what you have heard
    before, still serve us; it was to serve you came here.

Neoptolemus

    What would you have me do?

Odysseus

                       Ensnare
    the soul of Philoctetes with your words.
    When he asks who you are and whence you came,
    say you are Achilles' son; you need not lie.
    Say you are sailing home, leaving the Greeks
    and all their fleet, in bitter hatred. Say
    that they had prayed you, urged you from your home,   60
    and swore that only with your help
    could Troy be taken. Yet when you came and asked,
    as by your right, to have your father's arms,
    Achilles' arms, they did not think you worthy
    but gave them to Odysseus. Say what you will
    against me; do not spare me anything.

Nothing of this will hurt me; if you will not
do this, you will bring sorrow on all the Greeks.
If this man's bow shall not be taken by us,
you cannot sack the town of Troy.

Perhaps you wonder why you can safely meet him,   70
why he would trust you and not me. Let me explain.
You have come here unforced, unpledged by oaths,
made no part of our earlier expedition.
The opposite is true in my own case;
at no point can I deny his charge.
If, when he sees me, Philoctetes
still has his bow, there is an end of me,
and you too, for my company would damn you.
For this you must sharpen your wits, to become a thief
of the arms no man has conquered.

I know, young man, it is not your natural bent
to say such things nor to contrive such mischief.   80
But the prize of victory is pleasant to win.
Bear up: another time we shall prove honest.
For one brief shameless portion of a day
give me yourself, and then for all the rest
you may be called most scrupulous of men.

Neoptolemus
Son of Laertes, what I dislike to hear
I hate to put in execution.
I have a natural antipathy
to get my ends by tricks and stratagems.
So, too, they say, my father was. Philoctetes
I will gladly fight and capture, bring him with us,   90
but not by treachery. Surely a one-legged man
cannot prevail against so many of us!
I recognize that I was sent with you
to follow your instructions. I am loath
to have you call me traitor. Still, my lord,

I would prefer even to fail with honor
than win by cheating.

Odysseus
You are a good man's son.
I was young, too, once, and then I had a tongue
very inactive and a doing hand.
Now as I go forth to the test, I see
that everywhere among the race of men
it is the tongue that wins and not the deed.

Neoptolemus
What do you bid me do, but to tell lies?   100

Odysseus
By craft I bid you take him, Philoctetes.

Neoptolemus
And why by craft rather than by persuasion?

Odysseus
He will not be persuaded; force will fail.

Neoptolemus
Has he such strength to give him confidence?

Odysseus
The arrows none may avoid, that carry death.

Neoptolemus
Then even to encounter him is not safe?

Odysseus
Not if you do not take him by craft, as I told you.

Neoptolemus
Do you not find it vile yourself, this lying?

Osysseus
Not if the lying brings our rescue with it.

Neoptolemus
How can a man not blush to say such things?   110

Odysseus

When one does something for gain, one need not blush.

Neoptolemus

What gain for me that he should come to Troy?

Odysseus

His weapons alone are destined to take Troy.

Neoptolemus

Then I shall not be, as was said, its conqueror?

Odysseus

Not you apart from them nor they from you.

Neoptolemus

They must be my quarry then, if this is so.

Odysseus

You will win a double prize if you do this.

Neoptolemus

What? If I know, I will do what you say.

Odysseus

You shall be called a wise man and a good.

Neoptolemus

Well, then I will do it, casting aside all shame.   120

Odysseus

You clearly recollect all I have told you?

Neoptolemus

Yes, now that I have understood it.

Odysseus

                      Stay

and wait his coming here; I will go
that he may not spy my presence.
I will take with me to the ship this guard.
If you are too slow, I will send him back again,
disguise him as a sailor; Philoctetes
will never know him.
Whatever clever story he give you, then   130

fall in with it and use it as you need.
Now I will go to the ship and leave you in charge.
May Hermes, God of Craft, the Guide, for us
be guide indeed, and Victory and Athene,
the City Goddess, who preserves me ever.

(*Exit Odysseus.*)

Chorus
Sir, we are strangers, and this land is strange;
what shall we say and what conceal from this suspicious man?
Tell us.
For cunning that passes another's cunning
and a pre-eminent judgment lie with the prince,
in whose sovereign keeping is Zeus's holy scepter.   140
To you, young lord, all this has come,
all the power of your forefathers. Tell us now
what we must do to serve you.

Neoptolemus
Now—if you wish to see where he sleeps
on his crag at the edge—look, be not afraid.
But when the terrible wanderer returns,
be gone from the hut, but come to my beckoning.
Take your cues from me. Help when you can.

Chorus
Sir, this we have always done,   150
have kept a watchful eye over your safety.
But now
tell us what places he inhabits
and where he rests. It would not be amiss
for us to know this,
lest he attack us unawares.
Where does he live? Where does he rest?
What footpath does he follow? Is he in the house or not?

Neoptolemus
This, that you see, is his two-fronted house,
and he sleeps inside on the rock.   160

Chorus

    Where is he gone, unhappy creature?

Neoptolemus

                        I am sure
   he has gone to find food somewhere near here;
   stumbling, lame, dragging along the path,
   he is trying to shoot birds to prolong his miserable life.
   This indeed, they say, is how he lives.
   And no one comes near to cure him.

Chorus

    Yes, for my part I pity him:
    how unhappy, how utterly alone, always   170
    he suffers the savagery of his illness
    with no one to care for him,
    with no friendly face near him,
    but bewildered and distraught at each need as it comes.
    God pity him, how has he kept a grip on life?

    Woe to the contrivances of death-bound men,
    woe to the unhappy generations of death-bound men
    whose lives have known extremes!

    Perhaps this man is as well born as any,   180
    second to no son of an ancient house.
    Yet now his life lacks everything,
    and he makes his bed without neighbors
    or with spotted shaggy beasts for neighbors.
    His thoughts are set continually on pain and hunger.
    He cries out in his wretchedness;
    there is only a blabbering echo,
    that comes from the distance speeding
    from his bitter crying.   190

Neoptolemus

    I am not surprised at any of this:
    this is a God's doing, if I have any understanding.

These afflictions that have come upon him
are the work of Chryse, bitter of heart.
As for his present loneliness and suffering,
this, too, no doubt is part of the God's plan
that he may not bend against Troy
the divine invincible bow
until the time shall be fulfilled, at which it is decreed,
that Troy, as they say, shall fall to that bow.   200

Chorus
Hush.

Neoptolemus
     What is it?

Chorus
         Hush! I hear a footfall,
footfall of a man that walks painfully.
Is it here? Is it here?
I hear a voice, now I can hear it clearly,
voice of a man, crawling along the path,
hard put to it to move. It's far away,
but I can hear it; I can hear the sound well
the voice of a man wounded; it is quite clear now.

No more now, my son.   210

Neoptolemus
         No more of what?

Chorus
Your plots and plans. He is here, almost with us.
His is no cheerful marching to the pipe
like a shepherd with his flock.
No, a bitter cry.
He must have stumbled far down on the path,
and his moaning carried all the way here.
Or perhaps he stopped to look at the empty harbor,
for it was a bitter cry.

Philoctetes

Men, who are you that have put in, rowing   220
to a shore without houses or anchorage?
What countrymen may I call you without offense?
What is your people? Greeks, indeed, you seem
in fashion of your clothing, dear to me.
May I hear your voice? Do not be afraid
or shrink from such as I am, grown a savage.
I have been alone and very wretched,
without friend or comrade, suffering a great deal.
Take pity on me; speak to me; speak,
speak if you come as friends.
                              No—answer me.   230
If this is all
that we can have from one another, speech,
this, at least, we should have.

Neoptolemus

Sir, for your questions, since you wish to know,
know we are Greeks.

Philoctetes

                              Friendliest of tongues!
That I should hear it spoken once again
by such a man in such a place! My boy,
who are you? Who has sent you here? What brought you?
What impulse? What friendliest of winds?
Tell me all this, that I know who you are.

Neoptolemus

I am of Scyrus that the sea surrounds;
I am sailing home. My name is Neoptolemus,   240
Achilles' son. Now you know everything.

Philoctetes

Son of a father—that I loved so dearly—
and of a country that I loved, you that were reared
by that old man Lycomedes, what kind of venture
can have brought you to port here? Where did you sail from?

Neoptolemus
At present bound from Troy.

Philoctetes
From Troy? From Troy!
You did not sail with us to Troy at first.

Neoptolemus
You, then, are one that also had a share
in all that trouble?

Philoctetes
Is it possible
you do not know me, boy, me whom you see here?

Neoptolemus
I never saw you before. How could I know you?   250

Philoctetes
You never heard my name then? Never a rumor
of all the wrongs I suffered, even to death?

Neoptolemus
I never knew a word of what you ask me.

Philoctetes
Surely I must be vile! God must have hated me
that never a word of me, of how I live here,
should have come home through all the land of Greece.
Yet they that outraged God casting me away
can hold their tongues and laugh! While my disease
always increases and grows worse. My boy,
you are Achilles' son. I that stand here   260
am one you may have heard of, as the master
of Heracles' arms. I am Philoctetes
the son of Poias. Those two generals
and Prince Odysseus of the Cephallenians
cast me ashore here to their shame, as lonely
as you can see me now, wasting with my sickness
as cruel as it is, caused by the murderous bite
of a viper mortally dangerous.

I was already bitten when we put in here
on my way from sea-encircled Chryse.   270
I tell you, boy, those men cast me away here
and ran and left me helpless. They were happy
when they saw that I had fallen asleep on the shore
in a rocky cave, after a rough passage.
They went away and left me with such rags—
and few enough of them—as one might give
an unfortunate beggar and a handful of food.
May God give them the like!
Think, boy, of that awakening when I awoke
and found them gone; think of the useless tears
and curses on myself when I saw the ships—
my ships, which I had once commanded—gone,
all gone, and not a man left on the island,   280
not one to help me or to lend a hand
when I was seized with my sickness, not a man!
In all I saw before me nothing but pain;
but of that a great abundance, boy.

Time came and went for me. In my tiny shelter
I must alone do everything for myself.
This bow of mine I used to shoot the birds
that filled my belly. I must drag my foot,
my cursed foot, to where the bolt
sped by the bow's thong had struck down a bird.   290
If I must drink, and it was winter time—
the water was frozen—I must break up firewood.
Again I crawled and miserably contrived
to do the work. Whenever I had no fire,
rubbing stone on stone I would at last produce
the spark that kept me still in life.
A roof for shelter, if only I have fire,
gives me everything but release from pain.

Boy, let me tell you of this island.   300
No sailor by his choice comes near it.

There is no anchorage, nor anywhere
that one can land, sell goods, be entertained.
Sensible men make no voyages here.
Yet now and then someone puts in. A stretch
of time as long as this allows much to happen.
When they have come here, boy, they pity me—
at least they say they do—and in their pity
they have given me scraps of food and cast-off clothes;
that other thing, when I dare mention it,   310
none of them will—bringing me home again.

It is nine years now that I have spent dying,
with hunger and pain feeding my insatiable
disease. That, boy, is what they have done to me,
the two Atridae, and that mighty Prince
Odysseus. May the Gods that live in heaven
grant that they pay, agony for my agony.

Chorus
In this, I too resemble your other visitors.
I pity you, son of Poias.

Neoptolemus
                              I am a witness,
I also, of the truth of what you say.   320
I know it is true. I have dealt with those villains,
the two Atridae and the prince Odysseus.

Philoctetes
Are you, as well as I, a sufferer
and angry? Have you grounds against the Atridae?

Neoptolemus
Give me the chance to gratify my anger
with my hand some day!
Then will Mycenae know and Sparta know
that Scyrus, too, breeds soldiers.

Philoctetes

                                Well said, boy!
You come to me with a great hate against them.
Because of what?

Neoptolemus

                        I will tell you, Philoctetes—
for all that it hurts to tell it—
of how I came to Troy and what dishonor   330
they put upon me.
When fatefully Achilles came to die. . . .

Philoctetes

    O stop! tell me no more. Let me understand
this first. Is he dead, Achilles, dead?

Neoptolemus

    Yes, he is dead; no man his conqueror
but bested by a god, Phoebus the archer.

Philoctetes

    Noble was he that killed and he that died.
Boy, I am at a loss which to do first,
ask for your story or to mourn for him.

Neoptolemus

    God help you, I would think that your own sufferings
were quite enough without mourning for those of others.   340

Philoctetes

    Yes, that is true. Again, tell me your story
of how they have insulted you.

Neoptolemus

                           They came
for me, did great Odysseus and the man
that was my father's tutor, with a ship
wonderfully decked with ribbons. They had a story—
be it truth or lie—that it was God's decree
since he, my father, was dead, I and I only
should take Troy town.

This was their story. Sir, you can imagine
it did not take much time, when they had told it,   350
for me to embark with them.
Chiefly, you know, I was prompted by love of him,
the dead man. I had hope of seeing him
while still unburied. Alive I never had.
We had a favoring wind; on the second day
we touched Sigeion. As I disembarked,
all of the soldiers swarmed around me, blessed me,
swore that they saw Achilles alive again,
now gone from them forever. But he still lay
unburied. I, his mourning son, wept for him;   360
then, in a while, came to the two Atridae,
my friends, as it seemed right to do, and asked them
for my father's arms and all that he had else.
They needed brazen faces for their answer:
"Son of Achilles, all that your father had,
all else, is yours to take, but not his arms.
Another man now owns them, Laertes' son."
I burst into tears, jumped up, enraged,
cried out in my pain, "You scoundrels, did you dare
to give those arms that were mine to someone else   370
before I knew of it?" Then Odysseus
spoke—he was standing near me—"Yes, and rightly,"
he said, "they gave them, boy. For it was I
who rescued them and him, their former owner."
My anger got the better of me; I cursed him outright
with every insult that I knew, sparing none,
if he should take my arms away from me.
He is no way given to quarreling, but at this
he was stung by what I said. He answered:
"You were not where we were. You were at home,
out of the reach of duty. Since, besides,
you have so bold a tongue in your head, never   380
will you possess them to bring home to Scyrus."

« 61 »

There it was, abuse on both sides. But I lost
what should be mine and so sailed home. Odysseus,
that filthy son of filthy parents, robbed me.
Yet I do not blame him even so much as the princes.
All of a city is in the hand of the prince,
all of an army; unruly men become so
by the instruction of their betters.
This is the whole tale. May he that hates the Atridae
be as dear in the Gods' sight as he is in mine.   390

Chorus

Earth, Mountain Mother, in whom we find sustenance,
Mother of Zeus himself,
Dweller in great golden Pactolus,
Mother that I dread:
on that other day, too, I called on thee, Thou Blessed One,
Thou that rides on the Bull-killing Lions,
when all the insolence of the Atridae assaulted our Prince,
when they gave his arms, that wonder of the world,   400
  to the son of Laertes.

Philoctetes

You have sailed here, as it seems, with a clear tally;
your half of sorrow matches that of mine.
What you tell me rings in harmony. I recognize
the doings of the Atridae and Odysseus.
I know Odysseus would employ his tongue
on every ill tale, every rascality,
that could be brought to issue in injustice.
This is not at all my wonder, but that Ajax   410
the Elder should stand by, see and allow it.

Neoptolemus

He is no longer living, sir; never, indeed,
if he were, would they have robbed me of the arms.

Philoctetes

What! Is he, too, dead and gone?

Neoptolemus
    Yes, dead and gone. As such now think of him.

Philoctetes
    But not the son of Tydeus nor Odysseus
    whom Sisyphus once sold to Laertes,
    they will not die; for they should not be living.

Neoptolemus
    Of course, they are not dead; you may be sure
    that they are in their glory among the Greeks.   420

Philoctetes
    What of an old and honest man, my friend,
    Nestor of Pylos? Is he alive? He used
    to check their mischief by his wise advice.

Neoptolemus
    Things have gone badly for him. He has lost
    his son Antilochus, who once stood by him.

Philoctetes
    Ah!
    You have told me the two deaths that most could hurt me.
    Alas, what should I look for
    when Ajax and Antilochus are dead,
    and still Odysseus lives, that in their stead
    ought to be counted among the dead?   430

Neoptolemus
    A cunning wrestler; still, Philoctetes,
    even the cunning are sometimes tripped up.

Philoctetes
    Tell me, by the Gods, where was Patroclus,
    who was your father's dearest friend?

Neoptolemus
                            Dead, too.
    In one short sentence I can tell you this.
    War never takes a bad man but by chance,
    the good man always.

Philoctetes

       You have said the truth.
So I will ask you of one quite unworthy
but dexterous and clever with his tongue.   440

Neoptolemus

 Whom can you mean except Odysseus?

Philoctetes

 It is not he: there was a man, Thersites,
 who never was content to speak once only,
 though no one was for letting him speak at all.
 Do you know if he is still alive?

Neoptolemus

 I did not know him,
 but I have heard that he is still alive.

Philoctetes

 He would be; nothing evil has yet perished.
 The Gods somehow give them most excellent care.
 They find their pleasure in turning back from Death
 the rogues and tricksters, but the just and good
 they are always sending out of the world.   450
 How can I reckon the score, how can I praise,
 when praising Heaven I find the Gods are bad?

Neoptolemus

 For my own part, Philoctetes of Oeta,
 from now on I shall take precautions.
 I shall look at Troy and the Atridae both
 from very far off. I shall never abide
 the company of those where the worse man
 has more power than the better, where the good
 are always on the wane and cowards rule.
 For the future, rocky Scyrus will content me
 to take my pleasure at home.   460
 Now I will be going to my ship. Philoctetes,
 on you God's blessing and goodbye. May the Gods

recover you of your sickness, as you would have it!
Let us go, men, that when God grants us sailing
we may be ready to sail.

Philoctetes

                   Boy, are you going,

going now?

Neoptolemus

          Yes, the weather favors.
We must look to sail almost at once.

Philoctetes

My dear—I beg you in your father's name,
and in your mother's, in the name of all
that you have loved at home, do not leave me here   470
alone, living in sufferings you have seen
and others I have told you of.
I am not your main concern; give me a passing thought.
I know that there is horrible discomfort
in having me on board. Put up with it.
To such as you and your nobility,
meanness is shameful, decency honorable.
If you leave me here, it is an ugly story.
If you take me, men will say their best of you,
if I shall live to see Oetean land.
Come! One day, hardly one whole day's space   480
that I shall trouble you. Endure this much.
Take me and put me where you will,
in the hold, in the prow or poop, anywhere
where I shall least offend those that I sail with.
By Zeus himself, God of the Suppliants,
I beg you, boy, say "Yes," say you will do it.
Here I am on my knees to you, poor cripple,
for all my lameness. Do not cast me away
so utterly alone, where no one even walks by.
Either take me and set me safe in your own home,
or take me to Chalcedon in Euboea.

From there it will be no great journey for me   490
to Oeta or to ridgy Trachis or
to quick-flowing Spercheius,
and so you show me to my loving father.
For many a day I have feared that he is dead.
With those who came to my island I sent messages,
and many of them, begging him to come
and bring me home himself. Either he's dead,
or, as I rather think, my messengers
made little of what I asked them and hurried home.
Now in you I have found both escort and messenger;   500
bring me safe home. Take pity on me.
Look how men live, always precariously
balanced between good and bad fortune.
If you are out of trouble, watch for danger.
And when you live well, then consider the most
your life, lest ruin take it unawares.

Chorus
Have pity on him, prince.
He has has told us of a most desperate course run.
God forbid such things should overtake friends of mine.
And, prince, if you hate the abdominable Atridae   510
I would set their ill treatment of him
to his gain and would carry him
in your quick, well-fitted ship
to his home and so avoid offense before the face of God.

Neoptolemus
Take care that your assent is not too ready,
and that, when you have enough of his diseased company,   520
you are no longer constant to what you have said.

Chorus
No. You will never be able in this
to reproach me with justice.

Neoptolemus
                          I should be ashamed
to be less ready than you to render a stranger service.
Well, if you will then, let us sail. Let him
get ready quickly. My ship will carry him.

May God give us a safe clearance from this land
and a safe journey where we choose to go.

Philoctetes
God bless this day!   530
Man, dear to my very heart,
and you, dear friends, how shall I prove to you
how you have bound me to your friendship!
Let us go, boy. But let us first kiss the earth,
reverently, in my homeless home of a cave.
I would have you know what I have lived from,
how tough the spirit that did not break. I think
the sight itself would have been enough for anyone
except myself. Necessity has taught me,
little by little, to suffer and be patient.

Chorus
Wait! Let us see. Two men are coming.
One of them is of our crew, the other a foreigner.   540
Let us hear from them and then go in.

                    (*Enter the Sailor disguised as a Trader.*)

Trader
Son of Achilles, I told my fellow traveler here—
he with two others were guarding your ship—
to tell me where you were. I happened on you.
I had no intentions this way. Just by accident
I came to anchor at this island.
I am sailing in command of a ship outward bound
from Ilium, with no great company, for Peparethus—
a good country, that, for wine. When I heard
that all those sailors were the crew of your ship,   550

I thought I should not hold my tongue and sail on
until I spoke with you—and got my reward,
a fair one, doubtless. Apparently you do not know
much of your own affairs, nor what new plans
the Greeks have for you. Indeed, not only plans,
actions in train already and not slowly.

Neoptolemus

Thank you for your consideration, sir.
I will remain obliged to your kindness
unless I prove unworthy. Please tell me
what you have spoken of. I would like to know
what are these new plans of the Greeks.   560

Trader

Old Phoenix and the two sons of Theseus are gone,
pursuing you with a squadron.

Neoptolemus

                              Do they intend
to bring me back with violence or persuade me?

Trader

I do not know. I tell you what I heard.

Neoptolemus

Are Phoenix and his friends in such a hurry
to do the bidding of the two Atridae?

Trader

It is being done.
There is no delay about it. That you should know.

Neoptolemus

How is it that Odysseus was not ready
to sail as his own messenger on such
an errand? It cannot be he was afraid?

Trader

When I weighed anchor, he and Tydeus' son   570
were in pursuit of still another man.

Neoptolemus
> Who was this other man that Odysseus himself should seek him?

Trader
> There was a man—perhaps you will tell me first
> who this is; and say softly what you say.

Neoptolemus
> This, sir, is the famous Philoctetes.

Trader
>   Do not
> ask me any further questions. Get yourself out,
> as quickly as you can, out of this island.

Philoctetes
> What does he say, boy? Why in dark whispers
> does he bargain with you about me, this sailor?

Neoptolemus
> I do not know yet what he says, but he must say it,   580
> openly, whatever it is, to you and me and these.

Trader
> Son of Achilles, do not slander me,
> speaking of me to the army as a tattler.
> There's many a thing I do for them and in return
> get something from them, as a poor man may.

Neoptolemus
> I am the enemy of the Atridae. This
> is my greatest friend because he hates the Atridae.
> You have come to me as a friend, and so you must
> hide from me nothing that you heard.

Trader
> Well, watch what you are doing, sir.

Neoptolemus
>   I have.

Trader
> I put the whole responsibility
> squarely upon yourself.

Neoptolemus

Do so; but speak.   590

Trader

Well, then. The two I have spoken of,
the son of Tydeus and the Prince Odysseus,
are in pursuit of Philoctetes.
They have sworn, so help them God, to bring him with them
either by persuasion or by brute force.
And this all the Greeks heard clearly announced
by Prince Odysseus; for he was much surer
of success than was the other.

Neoptolemus

What can have made
the Atridae care about him after so long—
one whom they, years and years since, cast away?   600
What yearning for him came over them? Was it the Gods
who punish evil doings that now have driven them
to retribution for injustice?

Trader

I will explain all that. Perhaps you haven't heard.
There was a prophet of very good family,
a son of Priam indeed, called Helenus.
He was captured one night in an expedition
undertaken singlehanded by Odysseus,
of whom all base and shameful things are spoken,
captured by stratagem. Odysseus brought
his prisoner before the Greeks, a splendid prize.
Helenus prophesied everything to them   610
and, in particular, touching the fortress of Troy,
that they could never take it till they persuaded
Philoctetes to come with them and leave his island.
As soon as Odysseus heard the prophet say this,
he promised at once to bring the man before them,
for all to see—he thought, as a willing prisoner,
but, if not that, against his will. If he failed,

"any of them might have his head," he declared. My boy,
that is the whole story; that is why I urge you   620
and him and any that you care for to make haste.

Philoctetes
    Ah!
    Did he indeed swear that he would persuade me
    to sail with him, did he so, that utter devil?
    As soon shall I be persuaded, when I am dead,
    to rise from Death's house, come to the light again,
    as his own father did.

Trader
    I do not know about that. Well, I will be going now
    to my ship. May God prosper you both!

                                                        (Exit Trader.)

Philoctetes
    Is it not terrible, boy, that this Odysseus
    should think that there are words soft enough to win me,
    to let him put me in his boat, exhibit me
    in front of all the Greeks?   630
    No! I would rather listen to my worst enemy,
    the snake that bit me, made me into this cripple.
    But he can say anything, he can dare anything.
    Now I know that he will come here.
    Boy, let us go, that a great sea may sever
    us from Odysseus' ship.
    Let us go. For look, haste in due season shown
    brings rest and peace when once the work is done.

Neoptolemus
    When the wind at our prow falls, we can sail, no sooner.
    Now it is dead against us.   640

Philoctetes
    It is always fair sailing, when you escape evil.

Neoptolemus
    Yes, but the wind is against them, too.

Philoctetes
                                    For pirates
when they can thieve and plunder, no wind is contrary.

Neoptolemus
    If you will, then, let us go. Take from your cave
    what you need most and love most.

Philoctetes
    There are some things I need, but no great choice.

Neoptolemus
    What is there that you will not find on board?

Philoctetes
    A herb I have, the chief means to soothe my wound,
    to lull the pain to sleep.   650

Neoptolemus
                        Bring it out then.
    What else is there that you would have?

Philoctetes
    Any arrow
    I may have dropped and missed. For none of them
    must I leave for another to pick up.

Neoptolemus
    Is this, in your hands, the famous bow?

Philoctetes
                                    Yes, this,
    this in my hands.

Neoptolemus
                    May I see it closer,
    touch and adore it like a god?

Philoctetes
                            You may have it
    and anything else of mine that is for your good.

Neoptolemus
    I long for it, yet only with such longing   660

that if it is lawful, I may have it, else
let it be.

Philoctetes
            Your words are holy, boy. It is lawful.
for you have given me, and you alone,
the sight of the sun shining above us here,
the sight of my Oeta, of my old father, my friends.
You have raised me up above my enemies,
when I was under their feet. You may be confident.
You may indeed touch my bow, give it again
to me that gave it you, proclaim that alone
of all the world you touched it, in return
for the good deed you did. It was for that,
for friendly help, I myself won it first.   670

Neoptolemus
I am glad to see you and take you as a friend.
For one who knows how to show and to accept kindness
will be a friend better than any possession.
Go in.

Philoctetes
            I will bring you with me. The sickness in me
seeks to have you beside me.

Chorus
In story I have heard, but my eyes have not seen
him that once would have drawn near to Zeus's bed.
I have heard how he caught him, bound him on a running wheel,
Zeus, son of Kronos, invincible.
But I know of no other,   680
by hearsay, much less by sight, of all mankind
whose destiny was more his enemy when he met it
than Philoctetes', who wronged no one, nor killed
but lived, just among the just,
and fell in trouble past his deserts.
There is wonder, indeed, in my heart
how, how in his loneliness,

listening to the waves beating on the shore,
how he kept hold at all
on a life so full of tears.   690

He was lame, and no one came near him.
He suffered, and there were no neighbors for his sorrow
with whom his cries would find answer,
with whom he could lament the bloody plague
that ate him up.
No one who would gather
fallen leaves from the ground
to quiet the raging, bleeding sore,
running, in his maggot-rotten foot.   700
Here and there he crawled
writhing always—
suffering like a child
without the nurse he loves—
to what source of ease he could find
when the heart-devouring suffering gave over.

No grain sown in holy earth was his, nor other food
of all enjoyed by us, men who live by labor,
save when with the feathered arrows shot by the quick bow   710
he got him fodder for his belly.
Alas, poor soul,
that never in ten years' length
enjoyed a drink of wine
but looked always for the standing pools
and approached them.
But now he will end fortunate. He has fallen in
with the son of good men. He will be great, after it all.   720
Our prince in his seaworthy craft will carry him
after the fulness of many months, to his father's home
in the country of the Malian nymphs,
by the banks of the Spercheius,

where the hero of the bronze shield ascended
to all the Gods, ablaze in holy fire
above the ridges of Oeta.

Neoptolemus
Come if you will, then. Why have you nothing to say?   730
Why do you stand, in silence transfixed?

Philoctetes
Oh! Oh!

Neoptolemus
What is it?

Philoctetes
Nothing to be afraid of. Come on, boy.

Neoptolemus
Is it the pain of your inveterate sickness?

Philoctetes
No, no, indeed not. Just now I think I feel better.
O Gods!

Neoptolemus
Why do you call on the Gods with cries of distress?

Philoctetes
That they may come as healers, come with gentleness.
Oh! Oh!

Neoptolemus
What ails you? Tell me; do not keep silence.   740
You are clearly in some pain.

Philoctetes
I am lost, boy.
I will not be able to hide it from you longer.
Oh! Oh!
It goes through me, right through me!
Miserable, miserable!
I am lost, boy. I am being eaten up. Oh!

By God, if you have a sword, ready to hand, use it!
Strike the end of my foot. Strike it off, I tell you, now.
Do not spare my life. Quick, boy, quick.   750

(*A long silence.*)

Neoptolemus
What is this thing that comes upon you suddenly,
that makes you cry and moan so?

Philoctetes
Do you know, boy?

Neoptolemus
What is it?

Philoctetes
Do you know, boy?

Neoptolemus
What do you mean?
I do not know.

Philoctetes
Surely you know. Oh! Oh!

Neoptolemus
The terrible burden of your sickness.

Philoctetes
Terrible it is, beyond words' reach. But pity me.

Neoptolemus
What shall I do?

Philoctetes
Do not be afraid and leave me.
She comes from time to time, perhaps when she has had
her fill of wandering in other places.

Neoptolemus
You most unhappy man,
you that have endured all agonies, lived through them,   760
shall I take hold of you? Shall I touch you?

Philoctetes

    Not that, above everything. But take this bow,
    as you asked to do just now, until the pain,
    the pain of my sickness, that is now upon me, grows less.
    Keep the bow, guard it safely. Sleep comes upon me
    when the attack is waning. The pain will not end till then.
    But you must let me sleep quietly.
    If they should come in the time when I sleep,
    by the Gods I beg you do not give up my bow   770
    willingly or unwillingly to anyone.
    And let no one trick you out of it, lest you prove
    a murderer—your own and mine that kneeled to you.

Neoptolemus

    I shall take care; be easy about that. It shall not pass
    except to your hands and to mine. Give it to me now,
    and may good luck go with it!

Philoctetes

                     Here,
    take it, boy. Bow in prayer to the Gods' envy
    that the bow may not be to you a sorrow
    nor as it was to me and its former master.

Neoptolemus

    You Gods, grant us both this and grant us
    a journey speedy with a prosperous wind   780
    to where God sends us and our voyage holds.

Philoctetes

    An empty prayer, I am afraid, boy:
    the blood is trickling, dripping murderously
    from its deep spring. I look for something new.
    It is coming now, coming. Ah!
    You have the bow. Do not go away from me.
        Ah!
    O man of Cephallenia, would it were you,
    Would it were your breast that the pains transfix.
        Ah!   790

Agamemnon and Menelaus, my two generals,
would it were your two bodies that had fed
this sickness for as long as mine has. Ah!

Death, death, how is it that I can call on you,
always, day in, day out, and you cannot come to me?
Boy, my good boy, take up this body of mine
and burn it on what they call the Lemnian fire.   800
I had the resolution once to do this for another,
the son of Zeus, and so obtained the arms
that you now hold. What do you say?
What do you say? Nothing? Where are you, boy?

Neoptolemus
I have been in pain for you; I have been
in sorrow for your pain.

Philoctetes
No, boy, keep up your heart. She is quick in coming
and quick to go. Only I entreat you, do not
leave me alone.

Neoptolemus
Do not be afraid. We shall stay.   810

Philoctetes
You will?

Neoptolemus
You may be sure of it.

Philoctetes
Your oath,
I do not think it fit to put you to your oath.

Neoptolemus
I *may* not go without you, Philoctetes.

Philoctetes
Give me your hand upon it.

Neoptolemus
    Here I give it you,
    to remain.

Philoctetes
    Now—take me away from here—

Neoptolemus
                        What do you mean?

Philoctetes
                                    Up, up.

Neoptolemus
    What madness is upon you? Why do you look
    on the sky above us?

Philoctetes
                Let me go, let me go.

Neoptolemus
    Where?

Philoctetes
            Oh, let me go.

Neoptolemus
                    Not I.

Philoctetes
    You will kill me if you touch me.

Neoptolemus
    Now I shall let you go, now you are calmer.

Philoctetes
    Earth, take my body, dying as I am.
    The pain no longer lets me stand.   820

Neoptolemus
    In a little while, I think,
    sleep will come on this man. His head is nodding.
    The sweat is soaking all his body over,
    and a black flux of blood and matter has broken
    out of his foot. Let us leave him quiet, friends,
    until he falls asleep.

Chorus

Sleep that knows not pain nor suffering
kindly upon us, Lord,
kindly, kindly come.
Spread your enveloping radiance,
as now, over his eyes.
Come, come, Lord Healer.

Boy, look to your standing,
look to your going, look to your plans
for the future. Do you see? He sleeps.
What is it we are waiting to do?
Ripeness that holds decision over all things
wins many a victory suddenly.

Neoptolemus

Yes, it is true he hears nothing, but I see we have hunted in vain,
vainly have captured our quarry the bow, if we sail without him.
His is the crown of victory, him the God said we must bring.
Shame shall be ours if we boast and our lies still leave victory
    unwon.

Chorus

Boy, to all of this the God shall look.
Answer me gently;
low, low, whisper,
whisper, boy.
The sleep of a sick man has keen eyes.
It is a sleep unsleeping.

But to the limits of what you can,
look to this, look to this secretly,
how you may do it.
You know of whom I speak.
If your mind holds the same purpose touching this man,
the wise can see trouble and no way to cure it.
It is a fair wind, boy, a fair wind:
the man is eyeless and helpless,

830

840

850

outstretched under night's blanket—
asleep in the sun is good—
neither of foot nor of hand nor of anything is he master,   860
but is even as one that lies in Death's house.
Look to it, look if what you say
is seasonable. As far as my mind,
boy, can grasp it, best is the trouble taken
that causes the least fear.

Neoptolemus
   Quiet, I tell you! Are you mad? He is stirring,
   his eyes are stirring; he is raising his head.

Philoctetes
   Blessed the light that comes after my sleep,
   blessed the watching of friends.
   I never would have hoped this,
   that you would have the pity of heart to support   870
   my afflictions, that you should stand by me and help.
   The Atridae, those brave generals, were not so,
   they could not so easily put up with me.
   You have a noble nature, Neoptolemus,
   and noble were your parents. You have made light
   of all of this—the offense of my cries and the smell.
   And now, since it would seem I can forget
   my sickness for a while and rest, raise me yourself,
   raise me up, boy, and set me on my feet,
   that when my weariness releases me,
   we can go to the ship and sail without delay.   880

Neoptolemus
   I am glad to see you unexpectedly,
   eyes open, free of pain, still with the breath of life.
   With suffering like yours, all the signs pointed
   to your being dead. Now, lift yourself up.
   If you would rather, these men will lift you. They
   will spare no trouble, since you and I are agreed.

Philoctetes
> Thanks, boy. Lift me yourself, as you thought of it.
> Do not trouble them, let them not be disquieted   890
> before they need by the foul smell of me; living
> on board with me will try their patience enough.

Neoptolemus
> Very well, then; stand on your feet; take hold yourself.

Philoctetes
> Do not be afraid; old habit will help me up.

Neoptolemus
> Now is the moment. What shall I do from now on?

Philoctetes
> What is it, boy? Where are your words straying?

Neoptolemus
> I do not know what to say. I am at a loss.

Philoctetes
> Why are you at a loss? Do not say so, boy.

Neoptolemus
> It is indeed my case.

Philoctetes
> Is it disgust at my sickness? Is it this   900
> that makes you shrink from taking me?

Neoptolemus
> All is disgust when one leaves his own nature
> and does things that misfit it.

Philoctetes
> It is not unlike your father, either in word
> or in act, to help a good man.

Neoptolemus
> I shall be shown to be dishonorable:
> I am afraid of that.

Philoctetes
　　Not in your present actions. Your words make me hesitate.

Neoptolemus
　　Zeus, what must I do? Twice be proved base,
　　hiding what I should not, saying what is most foul?

Philoctetes
　　Unless I am wrong, here is a man who will　　　　　　910
　　betray me, leave me—so it seems—and sail away.

Neoptolemus
　　Not I; I will not leave you. To your bitterness,
　　I shall send you on a journey—and I dread this.

Philoctetes
　　What are you saying, boy? I do not understand.

Neoptolemus
　　I will not hide anything. You must sail to Troy
　　to the Achaeans, join the army of the Atridae.

Philoctetes
　　What! What can you mean?

Neoptolemus
　　　　　　　　　　　　Do not cry yet
　　until you learn.

Philoctetes
　　Learn what? What would you do with me?

Neoptolemus
　　First save you from this torture, then with you
　　go and lay waste the land of Troy.　　　　　　　　　920

Philoctetes
　　　　　　　　　　　　You would?
　　This is, in truth, what you intend?

Neoptolemus
　　　　　　　　　　　　Necessity,
　　a great necessity compels it. Do not be angry.

Philoctetes

Then I am lost. I am betrayed. Why, stranger,
have you done this to me? Give me back my bow.

Neoptolemus

That I cannot. Justice and interest
make me obedient to those in authority.

Philoctetes

You fire, you every horror, most hateful engine
of ruthless mischief, what have you done to me,
what treachery! Have you no shame to see me
that kneeled to you, entreated you, hard of heart?   930

You robbed me of my livelihood, taking my bow.
Give it back, I beg you, give it back, I pray, my boy!
By your father's Gods, do not take my livelihood.
He does not say a word,
but turns away his eyes. He will not give it up.

Caverns and headlands, dens of wild creatures,
you jutting broken crags, to you I raise my cry—
there is no one else that I can speak to—
and you have always been there, have always heard me,
Let me tell you what he has done to me, this boy,   940
Achilles' son. He swore to bring me home;
he brings me to Troy. He gave me his right hand,
then took and keeps my sacred bow,
the bow of Heracles, the son of Zeus,
and means to show it to the Argives,
as though in me he had conquered a strong man,
as though he led me captive to his power.
He does not know he is killing one that is dead,
a kind of vaporous shadow, a mere wraith.
Had I had my strength, he had not conquered me,
for, even as I am, it was craft that did it.
I have been deceived and am lost.
What can I do?

Give it back. Be your true self again. Will you not?   950
No word. Then I am nothing.

Two doors cut in the rock, to you again,
again I come, enter again, unarmed,
no means to feed myself! Here in this passage
I shall shrivel to death alone. I shall kill no more,
neither winged bird nor wild thing of the hills
with this my bow. I shall myself in death
be a feast for those that fed me. Those that I hunted
shall be my hunters now.
Life for the life I took, I shall repay
at the hands of this man that seemed to know no harm.   960

My curse upon your life!—but not yet still
until I know if you will change again;
if you will not, may an evil death be yours!

Chorus
What shall we do? Shall we sail? Shall we do as he asks?
Prince, it is you must decide.

Neoptolemus
A kind of compassion,
a terrible compassion, has come upon me
for him. I have felt for him all the time.

Philoctetes
Pity me, boy, by the Gods; do not bring on yourself
men's blame for your crafty victory over me.

Neoptolemus
What shall I do? I would I had never left
Scyrus, so hateful is what I face now.   970

Philoctetes
You are not bad yourself; by bad men's teaching
you came to practice your foul lesson. Leave it to others
such as it suits, and sail away. Give me my arms.

« 85 »

Neoptolemus
What shall we do, men?

(*Odysseus appears.*)

Odysseus
Scoundrel, what are you doing? Give me those arms.

Philoctetes
Who is this? Is that Odysseus' voice?

Odysseus

It is.
Odysseus certainly; you can see him here.

Philoctetes
Then I have been sold indeed; I am lost. It was he
who took me prisoner, robbed me of my arms.

Odysseus
Yes, I, I and no other. I admit that.   980

Philoctetes
Boy, give me back my bow, give it back to me.

Odysseus
That he will never
be able to do now, even if he wishes it.
And you must come with the bow, or these will
bring you.

Philoctetes
Your wickedness and impudence are without limit.
Will these men bring me, then, against my will?

Odysseus
Yes, if you do not come with a good grace.

Philoctetes
O land of Lemnos and all mastering brightness,
Hephaestus-fashioned, must I indeed bear this,
that he, Odysseus, drags me from you with violence?

Odysseus
It is Zeus, I would have you know, Zeus this land's ruler,
who has determined. I am only his servant.   990

« 86 »

Philoctetes

> Hateful creature,
> what things you can invent! You plead the Gods
> to screen your actions and make the Gods out liars.

Odysseus

> They speak the truth. The road must be traveled.

Philoctetes

> I say No.

Odysseus

> I say Yes. You must listen.

Philoctetes

> Are we slaves and not free? Is it as such
> our fathers have begotten us?

Odysseus

> No, but as equals
> of the best, with whom it is destined you must take Troy,
> dig her down stone by stone.

Philoctetes

> Never, I would rather suffer anything than this.
> There is still my steep and rugged precipice here.   1000

Odysseus

> What do you mean to do?

Philoctetes

> Throw myself down,
> shatter my head upon the rock below.

Odysseus

> Hold him. Take this solution out of his power.

Philoctetes

> Hands of mine, quarry of Odysseus' hunting,
> now suffer in your lack of the loved bowstring!
>
> You who have never had a healthy thought
> nor noble, you Odysseus, how you have hunted me,
> how you have stolen upon me with this boy

as your shield, because I did not know him, one
that is no mate for you but worthy of me,
who knows nothing but to do what he was bidden,   1010
and now, you see, is suffering bitterly
for his own faults and what he brought on me.
Your shabby, slit-eyed soul taught him step by step
to be clever in mischief against his nature and will.
Now it is my turn, now to my sorrow you have me
bound hand and foot, intend to take me away,
away from this shore on which you cast me once
without friends or comrades or city, a dead man among the living.

My curse on you! I have often cursed you before,
but the Gods give me nothing that is sweet to me.   1020
You have joy to be alive, and I have sorrow
because my very life is linked to this pain,
laughed at by you and your two generals,
the sons of Atreus whom you serve in this.
And yet, when you sailed with them, it was by constraint
and trickery, while I came of my own free will
with seven ships, to my undoing, I
whom they dishonored and cast away—
you say it was they that did it and they you.

But now why are you taking me? For what?
I am nothing now. To you all I have long been dead.   1030
God-hated wretch, how is it that now I am not
lame and foul-smelling? How can you burn your sacrifice
to God if I sail with you? Pour your libations?
This was your excuse for casting me away.

May death in ugly form come on you! It will so come,
for you have wronged me, if the Gods care for justice.
And I know that they do care for it, for at present
you never would have sailed here for my sake
and my happiness, had not the goad of God,

a need of me, compelled you.
Land of my fathers, Gods that look on men's deeds,   1040
take vengeance on these men, in your own good time,
upon them all, if you have pity on me!
Wretchedly as I live, if I saw them
dead, I could dream that I was free of my sickness.

Chorus
He is a hard man, Odysseus, this stranger,
and hard his words: no yielding to suffering in them.

Odysseus
If I had the time, I have much I could say to him.
As it is, there is only one thing. As the occasion
demands, such a one am I.
When there is a competition of men just and good,   1050
you will find none more scrupulous than myself.
What I seek in everything is to win
except in your regard: I willingly yield to you now.

Let him go, men. Do not lay a finger on him.
Let him stay here. We have these arms of yours
and do not need you, Philoctetes.
Teucer is with us who has the skill and I,
who, I think, am no meaner master of them
and have as straight an aim. Why do we need you?
Farewell: pace Lemnos. Let us go. Perhaps   1060
your prize will bring me the honor you should have had.

Philoctetes
What shall I do? Will you appear
before the Argives in the glory of my arms?

Odysseus
Say nothing further to me. I am going.

Philoctetes
Your voice has no word for me, son of Achilles?
Will you go away in silence?

Odysseus

Come, Neoptolemus.

Do not look at him. Your generosity
may spoil our future.

Philoctetes

You, too, men, will you go   1070
and leave me alone? Do you, too, have no pity?

Chorus

This young man is our captain. What he says to you
we say as well.

Neoptolemus (to the Chorus)

Odysseus will tell me
that I am full of pity for him. Still
remain, if he will have it so, as long
as it takes the sailors to ready the tackle
and until we have made our prayer to the Gods.
Perhaps, in the meantime, he will have better thoughts
about us. Let us go, Odysseus.
You, when we call you, be quick to come.   1080

(*Exeunt Odysseus and Neoptolemus.*)

Philoctetes

Hollow in the rock, hollow cave, sun-warmed, ice cold,
I was not destined, after all, ever to leave you.
Still with me, you shall be witness to my dying.
Passageway, crowded with my cries of pain,
what shall be, now again, my daily life with you?
What hope shall I find of food to keep my wretched life alive?   1090
Above me, in the clouds, down the shrill winds
the birds; no strength in me to stop them.

Chorus

It was you who doomed yourself,
man of hard fortune. From no other,
from nothing stronger, came your mischance.
When you could have chosen wisdom,

with better opportunity before you,
you chose the worse.   1100

Philoctetes

Sorrow, sorrow is mine. Suffering has broken me,
who must live henceforth alone from all the world,
must live here and die here;
no longer bringing home food nor winning
it with strong hands. Unmarked, the crafty words   1110
of a treacherous heart stole on me. Would I might see him,
contriver of this trap,
for as long as I am, condemned to pain.

Chorus

It was the will of the Gods
that has subdued you, no craft
to which my hand was lent.   1120
Turn your hate, your ill-omened curses, elsewhere.
This indeed lies near my heart,
that you should not reject my friendship.

Philoctetes

By the shore of the gray sea he sits and laughs at me.
He brandishes in his hand the weapon which kept me alive,
which no one else had handled. Bow that I loved,
forged from the hands that loved you, if you could feel,
you would see me with pity, successor to Heracles,   1130
that used you and shall handle you no more.
You have found a new master, a man of craft, and shall be bent
    by him.
You shall see crooked deceits and the face of my hateful foe,
and a thousand ill things such as he contrived against me.

Chorus

A man should give careful heed to say what is just;   1140
and when he has said it, restrain his tongue from rancor and taunt.
Odysseus was one man, appointed by many,
by their command he has done this, a service to his friends.

Philoctetes

Birds my victims, tribes of bright-eyed wild creatures,
tenants of these hills, you need not flee from me or my house.
No more the strength of my hands, of my bow, is mine.   1150
Come! It is a good time
to glut yourselves freely on my discolored flesh.
For shortly I shall die here. How shall I find means of life?
Who can live on air without any of all that life-giving earth sup-
        plies?   1160

Chorus

In the name of the gods, if there is anything that you hold in re-
        spect,
draw near to a friend that approaches you in all sincerity.
Know what you are doing, know it well.
It lies with you to avoid your doom.
It is a destiny pitiable to feed
with your body. It cannot learn how
to endure the thousand burdens with which it is coupled.

Philoctetes

Again, again you have touched my old hurt,   1170
for all that you are the best of those that came here.
Why did you afflict me? What have you done to me?

Chorus

What do you mean by this?

Philoctetes

Yes, you have hoped to bring me
to the hateful land of Troy.

Chorus

I judge that to be best.

Philoctetes

Then leave me now at once.

Chorus

Glad news, glad news.
I am right willing to obey you.
Let us go now to our places in the ship.   1180

Philoctetes

   No, by the God that listens to curses, do not go,
   I beseech you.

Chorus

         Be calm!

Philoctetes

            Friends, stay!
   I beg you to stay.

Chorus

        Why do you call on us?

Philoctetes

   It is the God, the God. I am destroyed.
   My foot, what shall I do with this foot of mine
   in the life I shall live hereafter?
   Friends, come to me again.   1190

Chorus

   What to do that is different
   from the tenor of your former bidding?

Philoctetes

   It is no occasion for anger
   when a man crazy with storms of sorrow
   speaks against his better judgment.

Chorus

   Unhappy man, come with us, as we say.

Philoctetes

   Never, never! That is my fixed purpose.
   Not though the Lord of the Lightning, bearing his fiery bolts,
   come against me, burning me
   with flame and glare.
   Let Ilium go down and all that under its walls   1200
   had the heart to cast me away, crippled!
   Friends, grant me one prayer only.

Chorus

            What is it you would seek?

Philoctetes

A sword, if you have got one,
or an ax or some weapon—give it me!

Chorus

What would you do with it?

Philoctetes

Head and foot,
head and foot, all of me, I would cut with my own hand.
My mind is set on death, on death, I tell you.

Chorus

Why this?   1210

Philoctetes

I would go seek my father.

Chorus

Where?

Philoctetes

In the house of death.
He is no longer in the light.
City of my fathers, would I could see you.
I who left your holy streams,
to go help the Greeks, my enemies,
and now am nothing any more.

Chorus

I should have been by now on my way to the ship,
did I not see Odysseus coming here   1220
and with him Neoptolemus.

(*Enter Odysseus and Neoptolemus in front of the cave, talking.*
Philoctetes withdraws into the cave.)

Odysseus (*to Neoptolemus*)

You have turned back, there is hurry in your step.
Will you not tell me why?

Neoptolemus

I go to undo the wrong that I have done.

Odysseus
A strange thing to say! What wrong was that?

Neoptolemus
I did wrong when I obeyed you and the Greeks.

Odysseus
What did we make you do that was unworthy?

Neoptolemus
I practiced craft and treachery with success.

Odysseus
On whom? Would you do some rash thing now?

Neoptolemus
Nothing rash. I am going to give something back.   1230

Odysseus
What? I am afraid to hear what you will say.

Neoptolemus
Back to the man I took it from, this bow.

Odysseus
You cannot mean you are going to give it back.

Neoptolemus
Just that. To my shame, unjustly, I obtained it.

Odysseus
Can you mean this in earnest?

Neoptolemus
                                                Yes, unless
it is not in earnest to tell you the truth.

Odysseus
What do you mean, Neoptolemus, what are you saying?

Neoptolemus
Must I tell you the same story twice or thrice?

Odysseus
I should prefer not to have heard it once.

Neoptolemus

You can rest easy. You have now heard everything. 1240

Odysseus

Then there is someone who will prevent its execution.

Neoptolemus

Who will that be?

Odysseus

The whole assembly
of the Greeks and among them I myself.

Neoptolemus

You are a clever man, Odysseus, but
this is not a clever saying.

Odysseus

In your own case
neither the words nor the acts are clever.

Neoptolemus

Still
if they are just, they are better than clever.

Odysseus

How can it be just to give to him again
what you won by my plans?

Neoptolemus

It was a sin,
a shameful sin, which I shall try to retrieve.

Odysseus

Have you no fear of the Greeks if you do this? 1250

Neoptolemus

I have no fear of anything you can do,
when I act with justice; nor shall I yield to force.

Odysseus

Then we shall fight
not with the Trojans but with you.

Neoptolemus
Let that be as it will.

Odysseus
               Do you see my hand,
reaching for the sword?

Neoptolemus
                  You shall see me do as much
and that at once.

Odysseus
            I will let you alone;
I shall go and tell this to the assembled Greeks,
and they will punish you.

Neoptolemus
                That is very prudent.
If you are always as prudent as this,
perhaps you will keep out of trouble.   1260

                        (*Exit Odysseus.*)

I call on you, Philoctetes, son of Poias,
come from your cave.

            (*Philoctetes appears at the mouth of the cave.*)

Philoctetes
               What cry is this at the door?
Why do you call me forth, friends? What would you have?
Ah! This is a bad thing. Can there be some fresh mischief
you come to do, to top what you have done?

Neoptolemus
Be easy. I would only have you listen.

Philoctetes
I am afraid of that.
I heard you before, and they were good words, too.
But they destroyed me when I listened.

Neoptolemus
Is there no place, then, for repentance?   1270

Philoctetes

You were just such a one in words when you stole my bow,
inspiring confidence, but sly and treacherous.

Neoptolemus

I am not such now. But I would hear from you
whether you are entirely determined
to remain here, or will you go with us?

Philoctetes

Oh, stop! You need not say another word.
All that you say will be wasted.

Neoptolemus

You are determined?

Philoctetes

More than words can declare.

Neoptolemus

I wish that I could have persuaded you.
If I cannot speak to some purpose, I have done.

Philoctetes

You will say it all   1280
to no purpose, for you will never win my heart
to friendship with you, who have stolen my life
by treachery, and then came and preached to me,
bad son of a noble father. Cursed be you all,
first the two sons of Atreus, then Odysseus,
and then yourself!

Neoptolemus

Do not curse me any more.
Take your bow. Here I give it to you.

Philoctetes

What can you mean? Is this another trick?

Neoptolemus

No. That I swear by the holy majesty
of Zeus on high!

Philoctetes
These are good words,   1290
if only they are honest.

Neoptolemus
The fact is plain.
Stretch out your hand; take your own bow again.

                                        (*Odysseus appears.*)

Odysseus
I forbid it, as the Gods are my witnesses,
in the name of the Atridae and the Greeks.

Philoctetes
Whose voice is that, boy? Is it Odysseus?

Odysseus
Himself and near at hand.
And I shall bring you to the plains of Troy
in your despite, whether Achilles' son
will have it so or not.

Philoctetes
You will rue your word
if this arrow flies straight.

Neoptolemus
                        No, Philoctetes, no!   1300
Do not shoot.

Philoctetes
                Let me go, let go my hand, dear boy.

Neoptolemus
I will not.

                                        (*Exit Odysseus.*)

Philoctetes
Why did you prevent me killing my enemy,
with my bow, a man that hates me?

Neoptolemus
This is not to our glory, neither yours nor mine.

Philoctetes

Well, know this much, that the princes of the army,
the lying heralds of the Greeks, are cowards
when they meet the spear, however keen in words.

Neoptolemus

Let that be. You have your bow. There is no further cause
for anger or reproach against me.

Philoctetes

None.

You have shown your nature and true breeding,   1310
son of Achilles and not Sisyphus.
Your father, when he still was with the living,
was the most famous of them, as now he is of the dead.

Neoptolemus

I am happy to hear you speak well of my father
and of myself. Now listen to my request.
The fortunes that the Gods give to us men
we must bear under necessity.
But men that cling wilfully to their sufferings
as you do, no one may forgive nor pity.   1320
Your anger has made a savage of you. You will not
accept advice, although the friend advises
in pure goodheartedness. You loathe him, think
he is your enemy and hates you.
Yet I will speak. May Zeus, the God of Oaths,
be my witness! Mark it, Philoctetes, write it in your mind.
You are sick and the pain of the sickness is of God's sending
because you approached the Guardian of Chryse,
the serpent that with secret watch protects
her roofless shrine to keep it from violation.
You will never know relief while the selfsame sun   1330
rises before you here, sets there again,
until you come of your own will to Troy,
and meet among us the Asclepiadae,

who will relieve your sickness; then with the bow
and by my side, you will become Troy's conqueror.

I will tell you how I know that this is so.
There was a man of Troy who was taken prisoner,
Helenus, a good prophet. He told us clearly
how it should be and said, besides, that all Troy   1340
must fall this summer. He said, "If I prove wrong
you may kill me."
Now since you know this, yield and be gracious.
It is a glorious heightening of gain.
First, to come into hands that can heal you,
and then be judged pre-eminent among the Greeks,
winning the highest renown among them, taking
Troy that has cost infinity of tears.

Philoctetes
Hateful life, why should I still be alive and seeing?
Why not be gone to the dark?
What shall I do? How can I distrust   1350
his words who in friendship has counseled me?
Shall I then yield? If I do so, how come
before the eyes of men so miserable?
Who will say word of greeting to me?
Eyes of mine, that have seen all, can you endure
to see me living with my murderers,
the sons of Atreus? With cursed Odysseus?
It is not the sting of wrongs past
but what I must look for in wrongs to come.
Men whose wit has been mother of villainy once   1360
have learned from it to be evil in all things.
I must indeed wonder at yourself in this.
You should not yourself be going to Troy
but rather hold me back. They have done you wrong
and robbed you of your father's arms. Will you go and help them
fight and compel me to the like?
No, boy, no; take me home as you promised.

Remain in Scyrus yourself; let these bad men
die in their own bad fashion. We shall both thank you,   1370
I and your father. You will not then, by helping
the wicked, seem to be like them.

Neoptolemus
What you say
is reasonable; yet I wish that you would trust
the Gods, my word, and, with me as friend, fare forth.

Philoctetes
What, to the plains of Troy, to the cursed sons
of Atreus with this suffering foot of mine?

Neoptolemus
To those that shall give you redress,
that shall save you and your rotting foot from its disease.

Philoctetes
Giver of dread advice, what have you said!   1380

Neoptolemus
What I see fulfilled will be best for you and me.

Philoctetes
And saying it, do you not blush before God?

Neoptolemus
Why should one feel ashamed to do good to another?

Philoctetes
Is the good for the Atridae or for me?

Neoptolemus
I am your friend, and the word I speak is friendly.

Philoctetes
How, then, do you wish to betray me to my enemies?

Neoptolemus
Sir, learn not to be defiant in misfortune.

Philoctetes
You will ruin me, I know it by your words.

Neoptolemus
Not I. You do not understand, I think.

Philoctetes .
Do I not know the Atridae cast me away?   1390

Neoptolemus
They cast you away; will, now again, restore you.

Philoctetes
Never, if of my will I must see Troy.

Neoptolemus
What shall we do, since I cannot convince you
of anything I say? It is easiest for me
to leave my argument, and you to live,
as you are living, with no hope of cure.

Philoctetes
Let me suffer what I must suffer.
But what you promised to me and touched my hand,
to bring me home, fulfil it for me, boy.
Do not delay, do not speak again of Troy   1400
I have had enough of sorrow and lamentation.

Neoptolemus
If you will then, let us go.

Philoctetes
Noble is the word you spoke.

Neoptolemus
Brace yourself, stand firm on your feet.

Philoctetes
To the limit of my strength.

Neoptolemus
How shall I avoid the blame of the Greeks?

Philoctetes
Give it no thought.

Neoptolemus
  What if they come and harry my country?

Philoctetes
  I shall be there.

Neoptolemus
  What help will you be able to give me?

Philoctetes
  With the bow of Heracles.

Neoptolemus
  Will you?

Philoctetes
  I shall drive them from it.

Neoptolemus
  If you will do what you say,
  come now; kiss this ground farewell, and come with me.

  (*Heracles appears standing on the rocks above the cave of Philoctetes.*)

Heracles
  Not yet, not until you have heard
  my words, son of Poias.
  I am the voice of Heracles in your ears;   1410
  I am the shape of Heracles before you.
  It is to serve you I come and leave my home among the dead.
  I come
  to tell you of the plans of Zeus for you,
  to turn you back from the road you go upon.
  Hearken to my words.

  Let me reveal to you my own story first,
  let me show the tasks and sufferings that were mine,
  and, at the last, the winning of deathless merit.   1420
  All this you can see in me now.
  All this must be your suffering too,
  the winning of a life to an end in glory,
  out of this suffering. Go with this man to Troy.

First, you shall find there the cure of your cruel sickness,
and then be adjudged best warrior among the Greeks.
Paris, the cause of all this evil, you shall kill
with the bow that was mine. Troy you shall take.
You shall win the prize of valor from the army
and shall send the spoils to your home,
to your father Poias, and the land of your fathers, Oeta.   1430
From the spoils of the campaign you must dedicate
some, on my pyre, in memory of my bow.

Son of Achilles, I have the same words for you.
You shall not have the strength to capture Troy
without this man, nor he without you,
but, like twin lions hunting together,
he shall guard you, you him. I shall send Asclepius
to Ilium to heal his sickness. Twice
must Ilium fall to my bow. But this remember,   1440
when you shall come to sack that town, keep holy in the sight of
   God.
All else our father Zeus thinks of less moment.
Holiness does not die with the men that die.
Whether they die or live, it cannot perish.

Philoctetes
   Voice that stirs my yearning when I hear,
   form lost for so long,
   I shall not disobey.

Neoptolemus
   Nor I.

Heracles
   Do not tarry then.
   Season and the tide are hastening you on your way.   1450

Philoctetes
   Lemnos, I call upon you:
   Farewell, cave that shared my watches,
   nymphs of the meadow and the stream,

the deep male growl of the sea-lashed headland
where often, in my niche within the rock,
my head was wet with fine spray,
where many a time in answer to my crying
in the storm of my sorrow the Hermes mountain sent its echo!   1460
Now springs and Lycian well, I am leaving you,
leaving you.
I had never hoped for this.
Farewell Lemnos, sea-encircled,
blame me not but send me on my way
with a fair voyage to where a great destiny
carries me, and the judgment of friends and the all-conquering
Spirit who has brought this to pass.

Chorus
Let us go all
when we have prayed to the nymphs of the sea   1470
to bring us safe to our homes.   1471

OEDIPUS AT COLONUS[1]

Translated by Robert Fitzgerald

INTRODUCTION

This play is generally dated about 408 or 407 B.C. The legendary action would fall between the end of *Oedipus the King* and the beginning of *Antigone*, but in a sense it is a sequel to both, for Sophocles seems to have drawn on his own characterization of Oedipus in the former and of Antigone, Ismene, and, in part, Creon in the latter.

The myth follows one variant concerning Oedipus' end, according to which, after being outcast from all other countries and his own, he was at last received by King Theseus of Athens at Sophocles' own birthplace, Colonus, in the territory of Attica. Creon pursued him there, tried to drag him away, and kidnapped his faithful daughters; Theseus intervened and rescued the girls. There Polyneices, his estranged son, came to ask his blessing and received only curses. There Oedipus miraculously passed from this world, to be established in the holy ground as a guardian spirit of Athens.

Notably rambling and loose in its construction, as compared with the other extant plays of Sophocles, *Oedipus at Colonus* nevertheless achieves its end—the reinstatement of a great man fallen. Oedipus enters at the very bottom of his fortunes, feeble, helpless, physically if not spiritually unclean. He leaves as an awe-inspiring, radiant hero. And it is all, stage by stage, made perfectly plausible, despite the melodramatic heroics of Theseus and the villainies of Creon. This is partly a sheer triumph of the art of writing dramatic speeches, which comes to a majestic climax in the messenger's tale of the passing of Oedipus, at the end.

CHARACTERS

Oedipus

Antigone

A Stranger

Ismene

Theseus

Creon

Polyneices

A Messenger

Chorus

OEDIPUS AT COLONUS

Long after he had left Thebes, the blinded OEDIPUS *came with* ANTIGONE
to the Attic deme of COLONUS, *where the oracle of Apollo had prophesied
that he was to die.*

SCENE: *Like the theatre, is in the open air. In the background is the grove
of the Furies at Colonus in Attica, about a mile northwest of
Athens. A statue or stele of Colonus, a legendary horseman and
hero, can be seen stage left. Stage right, a flat rock jutting out
among the trees of the grove. Downstage, center, another ridge of
rock.*

TIME: *Early afternoon of a day about twenty years after the action of*
King Oedipus.

SCENE I

> (*Oedipus, old, blind, bearded and ragged, but carrying
> himself well, enters stage right, led by Antigone.*)

Oedipus
    My daughter—daughter of the blind old man—
    Where, I wonder, have we come to now?
    What place is this, Antigone? What people?
    Who will be kind to Oedipus this evening
    And give the wanderer charity?

    Though he ask little and receive still less,   5
    It is sufficient:
                  Suffering and time,
    Vast time, have been instructors in contentment,
    Which kingliness teaches too.
                  But now, child,
    If you can see a place where we might rest,
    Some public place or consecrated park,   10
    Let me stop and sit down there.
    And then let us inquire where we may be.

As foreigners and strangers we must learn
From the local people, and do as they direct.

Antigone

Father, poor tired Oedipus, the towers
That crown the city still seem far away;   15
As for this place, it is clearly a holy one,
Shady with vines and olive trees and laurel;
Snug in their wings within, the nightingales
Make a sweet music.
      Rest on this rough stone.
It was a long road for an old man to travel.   20

Oedipus

Help me sit down; take care of the blind man.

Antigone

After so long, you need not tell me, father.

Oedipus

And now have you any idea where we are?

Antigone

This place I do not know; the city is Athens.

Oedipus

Yes, everyone we met has told us that.   25

Antigone

Then shall I go and ask?

Oedipus

Do, child, if there is any life near-by.

Antigone

Oh, but indeed there is; I need not leave you;
I see a man, now, not far away from us.

Oedipus

Is he coming this way? Has he started towards us?   30

        (*The Stranger enters, left.*)

Antigone

Here he is now.

Say what seems best to you,
Father; the man is here.

Oedipus

Friend, my daughter's eyes serve for my own.
She tells me we are fortunate enough to meet you,
And no doubt you will inform us—   35

Stranger

Do not go on;
First move from where you sit; the place is holy;
It is forbidden to walk upon that ground.

Oedipus

What ground is this? What god is honored here?

Stranger

It is not to be touched, no one may live upon it;
Most dreadful are its divinities, most feared,
Daughters of darkness and mysterious earth.   40

Oedipus

Under what solemn name shall I invoke them?

Stranger

The people here prefer to address them as Gentle
All-seeing Ones; elsewhere there are other names.

Oedipus

Then may they be gentle to the suppliant.
For I shall never leave this resting place.   45

Stranger

What is the meaning of this?

Oedipus

It was ordained;
I recognize it now.

Stranger

Without authority
From the city government I dare not move you;
First I must show them what it is you are doing.

Oedipus

    Friend, in the name of God, bear with me now!
    I turn to you for light; answer the wanderer.   50

Stranger

    Speak. You will not find me discourteous.

Oedipus

    What is this region into which I've come?

Stranger

    Whatever I can tell you, I will tell.
    This country, all of it, is blessed ground;
    The god of the sea loves it; in it the firecarrier   55
    Prometheus has his influence; in particular
    That spot you rest on has been called this earth's
    Doorsill of Brass, and buttress of great Athens.
    All men of this land claim descent from him
    Whose statue stands near-by: Colonus the horseman,
    And bear his name in common with their own.   60
    That is this country, stranger: honored less
    In histories than in the hearts of the people.

Oedipus

    Then people live in the land?

Stranger

                   Yes, certainly,
    The clan of those descended from that hero.   65

Oedipus

    Ruled by a king? Or do the people rule?

Stranger

    The land is governed from Athens, by Athens' king.

Oedipus

    And who is he whose word has power here?

Stranger

    Theseus, son of Aegeus, the king before him.

Oedipus

    Ah. Would someone then go to this king for me?   70

Stranger

To tell him what? Perhaps to urge his coming?

Oedipus

To tell him a small favor will gain him much.

Stranger

What service can a blind man render him?

Oedipus

All I shall say will be clear-sighted indeed.

Stranger

Listen, stranger: I wish you no injury;   75
You seem well-born, though obviously unlucky;
Stay where you are, exactly where I found you,
And I'll inform the people of what you say—
Not in the town, but here—it rests with them
To decide if you should stay or must move on.   80

(Exit Stranger, left.)

Oedipus

Child, has he gone?

Antigone

Yes, father. Now you may speak tranquilly,
For only I am with you.

Oedipus (praying)

                Ladies whose eyes
Are terrible: Spirits: upon your sacred ground
I have first bent my knees in this new land;   85
Therefore be mindful of me and of Apollo,
For when he gave me oracles of evil,
He also spoke of this:
                  A resting place,
After long years, in the last country, where
I should find home among the sacred Furies: 90
That there I might round out my bitter life,
Conferring benefit on those who received me,
A curse on those who have driven me away.

Portents, he said, would make me sure of this:
Earthquake, thunder, or God's smiling lightning; 95
But I am sure of it now, sure that you guided me
With feathery influence upon this road,
And led me here into your hallowed wood.

How otherwise could I, in my wandering,
Have sat down first with you in all this land, 100
I who drink not, with you who love not wine?

How otherwise had I found this chair of stone?
Grant me then, goddesses, passage from life at last,
And consummation, as the unearthly voice foretold;
Unless indeed I seem not worth your grace:
Slave as I am to such unending pain 105
As no man had before.
                              O hear my prayer,
Sweet children of original Darkness! Hear me,
Athens, city named for great Athena,
Honored above all cities in the world!
Pity a man's poor carcase and his ghost,
For Oedipus is not the strength he was. 110

Antigone

Be still. Some elderly men are coming this way,
Looking for the place where you are seated.

Oedipus

I shall be still. You get me clear of the path,
And hide me in the wood, so I may hear
What they are saying. If we know their temper 115
We shall be better able to act with prudence.
          (*Oedipus and Antigone withdraw into the grove.*)

CHORAL DIALOGUE

(*The Chorus enters from the left. Here, and throughout the
play, its lines may be taken by various members as
seems suitable.*)

Chorus

    Look for him. Who could he be? Where
    Is he? Where is the stranger
    Impious, blasphemous, shameless!   120
    Use your eyes, search him out!
    Cover the ground and uncover him!
              Vagabond!
    The old man must be a vagabond,
    Not of our land, for he'd never   125
    Otherwise dare to go in there,
    In the inviolate thicket
    Of those whom it's futile to fight,
    Those whom we tremble to name.
    When we pass we avert our eyes—
              Close our eyes!—   130
    In silence, without conversation,
    Shaping our prayers with our lips.
    But now, if the story is credible,
    Some alien fool has profaned it;
    Yet I have looked over all the grove and   135
              Still cannot see him;
    Cannot say where he has hidden.

              (*Oedipus comes forward from the wood.*)

Oedipus

    That stranger is I. As they say of the blind,
    Sounds are the things I see.

Chorus

              Ah!   140
    His face is dreadful! His voice is dreadful!

Oedipus

    Do not regard me, please, as a law-breaker.

Chorus

    Zeus defend us, who is this old man?

Oedipus

    One whose fate is not quite to be envied,

O my masters, and men of this land;   145
That must be evident: why, otherwise,
                    Should I need this girl
To lead me, her frailty to put my weight on?

Chorus

Ah! His eyes are blind!   150
And were you brought into the world so?
Unhappy life—and so long!
Well, not if I can help it,
Will you have this curse besides.—
                    Stranger! you   155
Trespass there! But beyond there,
In the glade where the grass is still,
Where the honeyed libations drip
In the rill from the brimming spring,
You must not step! O stranger,   160
It is well to be careful about it!
                    Most careful!
Stand aside and come down then!
There is too much space between us!
Say, wanderer, can you hear?   165
If you have a mind to tell us
Your business, or wish to converse with our council,
                    Come down from that place!
Only speak where it's proper to do so!

Oedipus

Now, daughter, what is the way of wisdom?   170

Antigone

We must do just as they do here, father;
We should give in now, and listen to them.

Oedipus

Stretch out your hand to me.

Antigone

                    There, I am near you.

Oedipus

   Sirs, let there be no injustice done me,
   Once I have trusted you, and left my refuge.   175

               (Led by Antigone, he starts downstage.)

Chorus

   Never, never, will anyone drive you away
   From rest in this land, old man!

Oedipus

   Shall I come further?

Chorus

               Yes, further.

Oedipus

   And now?

Chorus

               You must guide him, girl;   180
   You can see how much further to come.

Antigone

   Come with your blind step, father;
   This way; come where I lead you.

Chorus

   Though the land is strange, newcomer,
   You've weathered much; take heart;   185
   What the state has long held hateful,
   Hate, and respect what it loves.

Oedipus

   Lead me on, then, child,
   To where we may speak or listen respectfully;   190
   Let us not fight necessity.

Chorus

   Now! Go no further than that platform there,
   Formed of the natural rock.

Oedipus

   This?

Chorus
                    Far enough; you can hear us.

Oedipus
    Shall I sit down?

Chorus
                              Yes, sit there   195
    To the left on the ridge of the rock.

Antigone
    Father, this is where I can help you;
    You must keep step with me; gently now.

Oedipus
    Ah, me!

Antigone
    Lean your old body on my arm;   200
    It is I who love you; let yourself down.

Oedipus
    How bitter blindness is!

                    (*He is seated on the rock downstage, center.*)

Chorus
    Now that you are at rest, poor man,
    Tell us, what is your name?
    Who are you, wanderer?   205
    What is the land of your ancestors?

Oedipus
    I am an exile, friends; but do not ask me . . .

Chorus
    What is it you fear to say, old man?

Oedipus
    No, no, no! Do not go on   210
    Questioning me! Do not ask my name!

Chorus
    Why not?

Oedipus
　　　　My star was unspeakable.

Chorus
　　　　　　　　　Speak!

Oedipus
　My child, what can I say to them?

Chorus
　Answer us, stranger; what is your race,
　Who was your father?　　　　　　　　　　　　　　215

Oedipus
　God help me, what will become of me, child?

Antigone
　Tell them; there is no other way.

Oedipus
　Well, then, I will; I cannot hide it.

Chorus
　Between you, you greatly delay. Speak up!

Oedipus
　Have you heard of Laius' family?

Chorus
　　　　　　　　　Ah!　　　　　　　　　　　　　　220

Oedipus
　Of the race of Labdacidae?

Chorus
　　　　　　　Ah, Zeus!

Oedipus
　And ruined Oedipus?

Chorus
　　　　　　　　　You are he!

Oedipus
　Do not take fright from what I say—

Chorus
　Oh, dreadful!

Oedipus
          I am accursed.

Chorus
                    Oh, fearful!

Oedipus
     Antigone, what will happen now?   225

Chorus
     Away with you! Out with you! Leave our country!

Oedipus
     And what of the promises you made me?

Chorus
     God will not punish the man
     Who makes return for an injury:
     Deceivers may be deceived: 230
     They play a game that ends
     In grief, and not in pleasure.
     Leave this grove at once!
     Our country is not for you!
     Wind no further   235
     Your clinging evil upon us!

Antigone
     O men of reverent mind!
     Since you will not suffer my father,
     Old man though he is,
     And though you know his story—
     He never knew what he did—   240
     Take pity still on my unhappiness,
     And let me intercede with you for him.
     Not with lost eyes, but looking in your eyes
     As if I were a child of yours, I beg   245
     Mercy for him, the beaten man! O hear me!
     We are thrown upon your mercy as on God's;
                    Be kinder than you seem!
     By all you have and own that is dear to you:
     Children, wives, possessions, gods, I pray you!   250

For you will never see in all the world
      A man whom God has led
      Escape his destiny!

SCENE 2

Chorus

Child of Oedipus, indeed we pity you,
Just as we pity him for his misfortune;   255
But we tremble to think of what the gods may do;
We could not dare to speak more generously!

Oedipus

What use is reputation then? What good
Comes of a noble name? A noble fiction!
For Athens, so they say, excels in piety;   260
Has power to save the wretched of other lands;
Can give them refuge; is unique in this.
Yet, when it comes to me, where is her refuge?
You pluck me from these rocks and cast me out,
All for fear of a name!
               Or do you dread   265
My strength? my actions? I think not, for I
Suffered those deeds more than I acted them,
As I might show if it were fitting here
To tell my father's and my mother's story . . .
For which you fear me, as I know too well.

And yet, how was I evil in myself?   270
I had been wronged, I retaliated; even had I
Known what I was doing, was that evil?
Then, knowing nothing, I went on. Went on.
But those who wronged me knew, and ruined me.

Therefore I beg of you before the gods,   275
For the same cause that made you move me—
In reverence of your gods—give me this shelter,
And thus accord those powers what is theirs.
Think: their eyes are fixed upon the just,

Fixed on the unjust, too; no impious man   280
Can twist away from them forever.
Now, in their presence, do not blot your city's
Luster by bending to unholy action;
As you would receive an honest petitioner,
Give me, too, sanctuary; though my face   285
Be dreadful in its look, yet honor me!

For I come here as one endowed with grace
By those who are over Nature; and I bring
Advantage to this race, as you may learn
More fully when some lord of yours is here.   290
Meanwhile be careful to be just.

Chorus
                    Old man,
This argument of yours compels our wonder.
It was not feebly worded. I am content
That higher authorities should judge this matter.   295

Oedipus
And where is he who rules the land, strangers?

Chorus
In his father's city; but the messenger
Who sent us here has gone to fetch him also.

Oedipus
Do you think a blind man will so interest him
As to bring him such a distance?   300

Chorus
I do, indeed, when he has heard your name.

Oedipus
But who will tell him that?

Chorus
It is a long road, and the rumors of travellers
Have a way of wandering. He will have word of them;
Take heart—he will be here. Old man, your name   305

Has gone over all the earth; though he may be
At rest when the news comes, he will come quickly.

Oedipus

Then may he come with luck for his own city,
As well as for me. . . . The good befriend themselves.

Antigone

O Zeus! What shall I say? How interpret this?   310

Oedipus

Antigone, my dear child, what is it?

Antigone

                           A woman
Riding a Sicilian pony and coming towards us;
She is wearing the wide Thessalian sun-hat;
I don't know!   315
Is it or isn't it? Or am I dreaming?
I think so; yes!—No. I can't be sure. . . .

Ah, poor child,
It is no one else but she! And she is smiling   320
Now as she comes! It is my dear Ismene!

Oedipus

What did you say, child?
                              (*Ismene enters, with one Attendant.*)

Antigone

                           That I see your daughter!
My sister! Now you can tell her by her voice.

Ismene

O father and sister together! Dearest voices!
Now I have found you—how, I scarcely know—   325
I don't know how I shall see you through my tears!

Oedipus

Child, you have come?

Ismene

                           Father, how old you seem!

Oedipus
  Child, are you here?

Ismene
                    And such a time I had!

Oedipus
  Touch me, little one.

Ismene
                    I shall hold you both!

Oedipus
  My children . . . and sisters.

Ismene
                    Oh, unhappy people!   330

Oedipus
  She and I?

Ismene
                    And I with you, unhappy.

Oedipus
  But, child, why have you come?

Ismene
                    For your sake, father.

Oedipus
  You missed me?

Ismene
                    Yes; and I have news for you.
  I came with the one person I could trust.

Oedipus
  Why, where are your brothers? Could they not do it?   335

Ismene
  They are—where they are. It is a hard time for them.

Oedipus
  Ah! They behave as if they were Egyptians,
  Bred the Egyptian way! Down there, the men
  Sit indoors all day long, weaving;
  The women go out and attend to business.   340
  Just so your brothers, who should have done this work

Sit by the fire like home-loving girls,
And you two, in their place, must bear my hardships.

One, since her childhood ended and her body
Gained its power, has wandered ever with me,   345
An old man's governess; often in the wild
Forest going without shoes, and hungry,
Beaten by many rains, tired by the sun;   350
Yet she rejected the sweet life of home
So that her father should have sustenance.

And you, my daughter, once before came out,
Unknown to Thebes, bringing me news of all
The oracle had said concerning me;   355
And you remained my faithful outpost there,
When I was driven from that land.
                              But now,
What news, Ismene, do you bring your father?
Why have you left your house to make this journey?
You came for no light reason, I know that;
It must be something serious for me.   360

Ismene

I will pass over the troubles I have had
Searching for your whereabouts, father.
They were hard enough to bear; and I will not
Go through it all again in telling of them.
In any case, it is your sons' troubles   365
That I have come to tell you.
First it was their desire, as it was Creon's,
That the throne should pass to him; that thus the city
Should be defiled no longer: such was their reasoning
When they considered our people's ancient curse
And how it enthralled your pitiful family.   370
But then some fury put it in their hearts—
O pitiful again!—to itch for power:
For seizure of prerogative and throne;
And it was the younger and the less mature

Who stripped his elder brother, Polyneices,   375
Of place and kingship, and then banished him.

But now the people hear he has gone to Argos,
Into the valley land, has joined that nation,
And is enlisting friends among its warriors,
Telling them Argos shall honorably win   380
Thebes and her plain, or else eternal glory.
This is not a mere recital, father;
But terrible truth!
                            How long will it be, I wonder,
Before the gods take pity on your distress?

Oedipus

You have some hope then that they are concerned   385
With my deliverance?

Ismene

                            I have, father.
The latest sentences of the oracle . . .

Oedipus

How are they worded? What do they prophesy?

Ismene

That you shall be much solicited by our people
Before your death—and after—for their welfare.   390

Oedipus

And what could anyone hope from such as I?

Ismene

The oracles declare their strength's in you—

Oedipus

When I am finished, I suppose I am strong!

Ismene

For the gods who threw you down sustain you now.

Oedipus

Slight favor, now I am old! My doom was early.   395

Ismene

   The proof of it is that Creon is coming to you
   For that same reason, and soon: not by and by.

Oedipus

   To do what, daughter? Tell me about this.

Ismene

   To settle you near the land of Thebes, and so
   Have you at hand; but you may not cross the border.   400

Oedipus

   What good am I to them outside the country?

Ismene

   It is merely that if your burial were unlucky,
   That would be perilous for them.

Oedipus

                Ah, then!
   No god's assistance is needed in comprehending.

Ismene

   Therefore they want to keep you somewhere near,
   Just at the border, where you'll not be free.   405

Oedipus

   And will they compose my shade with Theban dust?

Ismene

   Ah, father! No. Your father's blood forbids it.

Oedipus

   Then they shall never hold me in their power!

Ismene

   If so, some day it will be bitter for them.

Oedipus

   How will that be, my child?

Ismene

               When they shall stand   410
   Where you are buried, and feel your anger there.

Oedipus

What you have said—from whom did you hear it, child?

Ismene

The envoys told me when they returned from Delphi.

Oedipus

Then all this about me was spoken there?

Ismene

According to those men, just come to Thebes.   415

Oedipus

Has either of my sons had word of this?

Ismene

They both have, and they understand it well.

Oedipus

The scoundrels! So they knew all this, and yet
Would not give up the throne to have me back?

Ismene

It hurts me to hear it, but I can't deny it.   420

Oedipus

Gods!
Put not their fires of ambition out!
Let the last word be mine upon this battle
They are about to join, with the spears lifting!
I'd see that the one who holds the sceptre now   425
Would not have power long, nor would the other,
The banished one, return!

                These were the two
Who saw me in disgrace and banishment
And never lifted a hand for me. They heard me
Howled from the country, heard the thing proclaimed!   430

And will they say I wanted exile then,
An appropriate clemency, granted by the state?
That is all false! The truth is that at first

My mind was a boiling caldron; nothing so sweet
As death, death by stoning, could have been given me;   435
Yet no one there would grant me that desire.
It was only later, when my madness cooled,
And I had begun to think my rage excessive,
My punishment too great for what I had done;
Then it was that the city—in its good time!—   440
Decided to be harsh, and drove me out.
They could have helped me then; they could have
Helped him who begot them! Would they do it?
For lack of a little word from that fine pair
Out I went, like a beggar, to wander forever!   445
Only by grace of these two girls, unaided,
Have I got food or shelter or devotion;
The others held their father of less worth
Than sitting on a throne and being king.

Well, they shall never win me in their fight!   450
Nor will they profit from the rule of Thebes.
I am sure of that; I have heard the prophecies
Brought by this girl; I think they fit those others
Spoken so long ago, and now fulfilled.
So let Creon be sent to find me: Creon,   455
Or any other of influence in the state.
If you men here consent—as do those powers
Holy and awful, the spirits of this place—
To give me refuge, then shall this city have
A great savior; and woe to my enemies!   460

Chorus
Oedipus: you are surely worth our pity:
You, and your children, too. And since you claim
Also to be a savior of our land,
I'd like to give you counsel for good luck.

Oedipus
Dear friend! I'll do whatever you advise.   465

Chorus
  Make expiation to these divinities
  Whose ground you violated when you came.

Oedipus
  In what way shall I do so? Tell me, friends.

Chorus
  First you must bring libations from the spring
  That runs forever; and bring them with clean hands.   470

Oedipus
  And when I have that holy water, then?

Chorus
  There are some bowls there, by a skillful potter;
  Put chaplets round the brims, over the handles.

Oedipus
  Of myrtle springs, or woolen stuff, or what?

Chorus
  Take the fleeces cropped from a young lamb.   475

Oedipus
  Just so; then how must I perform the rite?

Chorus
  Facing the quarter of the morning light,
  Pour your libations out.

Oedipus
  Am I to pour them from the bowls you speak of?

Chorus
  In three streams, yes; the last one, empty it.

Oedipus
  With what should it be filled? Tell me this, too.   480

Chorus
  With water and honey; but with no wine added.

Oedipus

And when the leaf-dark earth receives it?

Chorus

Lay three times nine young shoots of olive on it
With both your hands; meanwhile repeat this prayer:

Oedipus

This I am eager to hear: it has great power.   485

Chorus

That as we call them Eumenides,
Which means the gentle of heart,
May they accept with gentleness
The suppliant and his wish.

So you, or he who prays for you, address them;

But do not speak aloud or raise a cry;
Then come away, and do not turn again.   490
If you will do all this, I shall take heart
And stand up for you; otherwise, O stranger,
I should be seriously afraid for you.

Oedipus

Children, you hear the words of these good people?

Antigone

Yes; now tell us what we ought to do.

Oedipus

It need not be performed by me; I'm far   495
From having the strength or sight for it—I have neither.
Let one of you go and carry out the ritual.
One soul, I think, often can make atonement
For many others, if it be sincere.
Now do it quickly.—Yet do not leave me alone!   500
I could not move without the help of someone.

Ismene

I'll go and do it. But where am I to go?
Where shall I find the holy place, I wonder?

Chorus

On the other side of the wood, girl. If you need it,   505
You may get help from the attendant there.

Ismene

I am going now. Antigone, you'll stay
And care for father. Even if it were hard,
I should not think it so, since it is for him.

(*Ismene goes out, right. The chorus draws nearer to Oedipus.*)

CHORAL DIALOGUE

Chorus

What evil things have slept since long ago   510
    It is not sweet to awaken;
    And yet I long to be told—

Oedipus

                    What?

Chorus

Of that heartbreak for which there was no help,
    The pain you have had to suffer.

Oedipus

    For kindness' sake, do not open   515
    My old wound, and my shame.

Chorus

It is told everywhere, and never dies;
    I only want to hear it truly told.

Oedipus

Ah! Ah!

Chorus

                    Consent I beg you;
Give me my wish, and I shall give you yours.   520

Oedipus

I had to face a thing most terrible,
    Not willed by me, I swear;
    I would have abhorred it all.

Chorus

So?

Oedipus

Though I did not know, Thebes married me to evil;   525
Fate and I were joined there.

Chorus

Then it was indeed your mother
With whom the thing was done?

Oedipus

Ah! It is worse than death to have to hear it!
Strangers! Yes: and these two girls of mine . . .   530

Chorus

Go on—

Oedipus

These luckless two

Were given birth by her who gave birth to me.

Chorus

These then are daughters; they are also—

Oedipus

Sisters: yes, their father's sisters . . .   535

Chorus

Ah, pity!

Oedipus

Pity, indeed. What throngs

Of pities come into my mind!

Chorus

You suffered—

Oedipus

Yes, unspeakably.

Chorus

You sinned—

Oedipus

No, I did not sin!

Chorus
>   How not?

Oedipus
>   I thought
> Of her as my reward. Ah, would I had never won it!   540
> Would I had never served the State that day!

Chorus
> Unhappy man—and you also killed—

Oedipus
> What is it now? What are you after?

Chorus
> Killed your father!

Oedipus
>   God in heaven!
> You strike again where I am hurt.

Chorus
> You killed him.

Oedipus
>   Killed him. Yet, there is—   545

Chorus
> What more?

Oedipus
>   A just extenuation.
>   This:
> I did not know him; and he wished to murder me.
> Before the law—before God—I am innocent!

> *(The Chorus turns at the approach of Theseus.)*

SCENE 3

Chorus
> The king is coming! Aegeus' eldest son,
> Theseus: news of you has brought him here.   550

> *(Theseus enters with soldiers, left.)*

Theseus

In the old time I often heard men tell
Of the bloody extinction of your eyes.
Even if on my way I were not informed,
I'd recognize you, son of Laius.
The garments and the tortured face   555
Make plain your identity. I am sorry for you.
And I should like to know what favor here
You hope for from the city and from me:
Both you and your unfortunate companion.
Tell me. It would be something dire indeed   560
To make me leave you comfortless; for I
Too was an exile. I grew up abroad,
And in strange lands I fought as few men have
With danger and with death.
Therefore no wanderer shall come, as you do,   565
And be denied my audience or aid.
I know I am only a man; I have no more
To hope for in the end than you have.

Oedipus

Theseus, in those few words your nobility
Is plain to me. I need not speak at length;   570
You have named me and my father accurately,
Spoken with knowledge of my land and exile.
There is, then, nothing left for me to tell
But my desire; and then the tale is ended.

Theseus

Tell me your wish, then; let me hear it now.   575

Oedipus

I come to give you something, and the gift
Is my own beaten self: no feast for the eyes;
Yet in me is a more lasting grace than beauty.

Theseus

What grace is this you say you bring to us?

Oedipus
In time you'll learn, but not immediately.   580

Theseus
How long, then, must we wait to be enlightened?

Oedipus
Until I am dead, and you have buried me.

Theseus
Your wish is burial? What of your life meanwhile?
Have you forgotten that?—or do you care?

Oedipus
It is all implicated in my burial.   585

Theseus
But this is a brief favor you ask of me.

Oedipus
See to it, nevertheless! It is not simple.

Theseus
You mean I shall have trouble with your sons?

Oedipus
Those people want to take me back there now.

Theseus
Will you not go? Is exile admirable?   590

Oedipus
No. When I would have returned, they would not have it.

Theseus
What childishness! You are surely in no position—

Oedipus
When you know me, rebuke me; not till then!

Theseus
Well, tell me more. I must not speak in ignorance.

Oedipus
Theseus, I have been wounded more than once.   595

Theseus

    Is it your family's curse that you refer to?

Oedipus

    Not merely that; for all Greece buzzes with it.

Theseus

    Then what is the wound that is so pitiless?

Oedipus

    Think how it is with me. I was expelled
    From my own land by my own sons; and now,   600
    As a parricide, my return is not allowed.

Theseus

    How can they summon you, if this is so?

Oedipus

    The sacred oracle compels them to.

Theseus

    They fear some punishment from his forebodings?

Oedipus

    They fear they will be struck down in this land!   605

Theseus

    And how could war arise between these nations?

Oedipus

    Most gentle son of Aegeus! The immortal
    Gods alone have neither age nor death!
    All other things almighty Time disquiets.
    Earth wastes away; the body wastes away;   610
    Faith dies; distrust is born.
    And imperceptibly the spirit changes
    Between a man and his friend, or between two cities.
    For some men soon, for others in later time,
    Their pleasure sickens; or love comes again.   615
    And so with you and Thebes: the sweet season
    Holds between you now; but time goes on,
    Unmeasured Time, fathering numberless

Nights, unnumbered days: and on one day
They'll break apart with spears this harmony—   620
All for a trivial word.
And then my sleeping and long-hidden corpse,
Cold in the earth, will drink hot blood of theirs,
If Zeus endures; if his son's word is true . . .

However: there's no felicity in speaking
Of hidden things. Let me come back to this: 625
Be careful that you keep your word to me;
For if you do you'll never say of Oedipus
That he was given refuge uselessly—
Or if you say it, then the gods have lied.

Chorus

My lord: before you came this man gave promise
Of having power to make his words come true.   630

Theseus

Who would reject his friendship? Is he not
One who would have, in any case, an ally's
Right to our hospitality?
Moreover he has asked grace of our deities,
And offers no small favor in return.   635
As I value that favor, I shall not refuse
This man's desire; I declare him a citizen.

And if it should please our friend to remain here,
I direct you to take care of him;
Or else he may come with me.
                            Whatever you choose,
Oedipus, we shall be happy to accord.   640
You know your own needs best; I accede to them.

Oedipus

May God bless men like these!

Theseus

What do you say then? Shall it be my house?

Oedipus
If it were right for me. But the place is here . . .

Theseus
And what will you do here?—Not that I oppose you.   645

Oedipus
Here I shall prevail over those who banished me.

Theseus
Your presence, as you say, is a great blessing.

Oedipus
If you are firm in doing what you promise.

Theseus
You can be sure of me; I'll not betray you.

Oedipus
I'll not ask pledges, as I would of scoundrels.   650

Theseus
You'd get no more assurance than by my word.

Oedipus
I wonder how you will behave?

Theseus
                    You fear?

Oedipus
That men will come—

Theseus
                    These men will attend to them.

Oedipus
Look: when you leave me—

Theseus
                    I know what to do!

Oedipus
I am oppressed by fear!

Theseus
                    I feel no fear.   655

Oedipus

You do not know the menace!

Theseus

                I do know
No man is going to take you against my will.
Angry men are liberal with threats
And bluster generally. When the mind
Is master of itself, threats are no matter. 660
These people may have dared to talk quite fiercely
Of taking you; perhaps, as I rather think,
They'll find a sea of troubles in the way.
Therefore I should advise you to take heart.
Even aside from me and my intentions,
Did not Apollo send and guide you here? 665
However it may be, I can assure you,
While I'm away, my name will be your shield.

(Exit Theseus and soldiers. The Chorus turns to the audience.)

CHORAL POEM

Chorus

The land beloved of horsemen, fair
Colonus takes a guest;
He shall not seek another home, 670
For this, in all the earth and air,
Is most secure and loveliest.

In the god's untrodden vale
Where leaves and berries throng,
And wine-dark ivy climbs the bough,
The sweet, sojourning nightingale
Murmurs all day long. 675

No sun nor wind may enter there
Nor the winter's rain;
But ever through the shadow goes
Dionysus reveler,
Immortal maenads in his train. 680

« 142 »

Here with drops of heaven's dews
At daybreak all the year,
The clusters of narcissus bloom,
Time-hallowed garlands for the brows
Of those great ladies whom we fear.   685

The crocus like a little sun
Blooms with its yellow ray;
The river's fountains are awake,
And his nomadic streams that run
Unthinned forever, and never stay;   690

But like perpetual lovers move
On the maternal land.
And here the choiring Muses come,
And the divinity of love
With the gold reins in her hand.

(*The Chorus may now shift its grouping or otherwise
indicate a change of theme.*)

Chorus

And our land has a thing unknown
On Asia's sounding coast   695
Or in the sea-surrounded west
Where Agamemnon's race has sway:
The olive, fertile and self-sown,
The terror of our enemies
That no hand tames nor tears away—
The blessed tree that never dies!—
But it will mock the swordsman in his rage.

Ah, how it flourishes in every field,
Most beautifully here!   700
The gray-leafed tree, the children's nourisher!
No young man nor one partnered by his age
Knows how to root it out nor make
Barren its yield;
For Zeus the Father smiles on it with sage

Eyes that forever are awake,   705
And Pallas watches with her sea-pale eyes.

Last and grandest praise I sing
To Athens, nurse of men,
For her great pride and for the splendor
Destiny has conferred on her.   710
Land from which fine horses spring!
Land where foals are beautiful!
Land of the sea and the sea-farer!
Upon whose lovely littoral
The god of the sea moves, the son of Time.

That lover of our land I praise again,
Who found our horsemen fit
For first bestowal of the curb and bit,   715
To discipline the stallion in his prime;
And strokes to which our oarsmen sing,
Well-fitted, oak and men,
Whose long sea-oars in wondrous rhyme
Flash from the salt foam, following
The hundred-footed sea-wind and the gull.

*(At the conclusion of this, Antigone is standing stage
right, looking off-stage attentively.)*

Scene 4

Antigone
Land so well spoken of and praised so much!   720
Now is the time to show those words are true.

Oedipus
What now, my child?

Antigone (returning to him)
                                A man is coming towards us,
And it is Creon—not unaccompanied, father.

Oedipus
Most kindly friends! I hope you may give proof,
And soon, of your ability to protect me!   725

Chorus

> Don't be afraid: you'll see. I may be old,
> But the nation's strength has not grown old.

> *(Enter Creon, right, with guards.)*

Creon

> Gentlemen, and citizens of this land:
> I can see from your eyes that my arrival
> Has been a cause of sudden fear to you;   730
> Do not be fearful. And say nothing hostile!
> I have not come for any hostile action,
> For I am old, and know this city has
> Power, if any city in Hellas has.

> But for this man here: I, despite my age,   735
> Am sent to bring him to the land of Thebes.
> This is not one man's mission, but was ordered
> By the whole Theban people. I am their emissary
> Because it fell to me as a relative
> To mourn his troubles more than anyone.

> So, now, poor Oedipus, come home.   740
> You have heard my message. The people of the city
> Are right in summoning you—I most of all,
> For most of all, unless I am worst of men,
> I grieve for your unhappiness, old man.
> I see you ravaged as you are, a stranger   745
> Everywhere, never at rest,
> With only a girl to serve you in your need.—
> I never thought she'd fall to such indignity,
> Poor child! And yet she has;   750
> Forever tending you, leading a beggar's
> Life with you; a grown-up girl who knows
> Nothing of marriage; whoever comes can take her. . . .

> Is not this a disgrace? I weep to see it!
> Disgrace for you, for me, for all our people!
> We cannot hide what is so palpable,   755
> But you, if you will listen to me, Oedipus—

And in the name of your father's gods, listen!—
Bury the whole thing now; agree with me
To go back to your city and your home!

Take friendly leave of Athens, for she deserves it;
But you should have more reverence for Thebes,
Since long ago she was your kindly nurse.   760

Oedipus

You brazen rascal! Playing your rascal's tricks
In righteous speeches, as you always would!
Why do you try it? How can you think to take me
Into that snare I should so hate if taken?

That time when I was sick with my private   765
Agony: when I would lightly have left the earth—
You had no mind to give me what I wanted!
But when at long last I had had my fill
Of rage and grief, and in my quiet house
Began to find some comfort: that was the time
You chose to rout me out.   770
How precious was this kinship to you then?
It is the same thing now: you see this city
And all its people being kind to me,
So you attempt to coax me away from them!
A cruel thing, for all your soothing words.

What pleasure is there in being amiable   775
To those who do not want your amiability?

Suppose that when you wanted something terribly
A man should neither grant it you nor give
Sympathy even; but later when you were glutted
With all your heart's desire, should give it then,
When charity was no charity at all?
Would you not think the kindness somewhat hollow?   780
That is the sort of kindness you offer me:
Generous in words, but in reality evil.

Now I will tell these men, and prove you evil.
You come to take me, but not to take me home;
Rather to settle me outside the city
So that the city may escape my curse,   785
Escape from punishment by Athens.
                              Yes;
But you'll not have it. What you'll have is this:
My vengeance active in that land forever;
And what my sons will have of my old kingdom
Is just so much room as they need to die in!   790

Now who knows better the destiny of Thebes?
I do, for I have had the best informants:
Apollo, and Zeus himself who is his father.
And yet you come here with your fraudulent speech
All whetted up! The more you talk, the more   795
Harm, not good, you'll get by it!—
However, I know you'll never believe that.—

Only leave us! Let us live here in peace!
Is it a bad life, if it gives us pleasure?

Creon

Which of us do you consider is more injured   800
By talk like this? You hurt only yourself.

Oedipus

I am perfectly content, so long as you
Can neither wheedle me nor fool these others.

Creon

Unhappy man! Shall it be plain that time
Brings you no wisdom? that you shame your age?   805

Oedipus

What repartee! I know no honest man
Able to speak so well under all conditions!

Creon

To speak much is one thing; to speak to the point's another!

Oedipus

As if you spoke so little but so fittingly!

Creon

No, not fittingly for a mind like yours! 810

Oedipus

Go away! I speak for these men also!
Stop busybodying here where I must live!

Creon

I call on these—not you!—as witnesses
Of what rejoinder you have made to friends.—
If I ever take you—

Oedipus

With these men fighting for me,
Who is going to take me by violence? 815

Creon

You'll have pain enough without that, I promise you!

Oedipus

What are you up to? What is behind that brag?

Creon

Your two daughters: one of them I have just now
Had seized and carried off, and I'll take this one!

Oedipus

Ah!

Creon

You'll soon have better reason to groan about it! 820

Oedipus

You have my child?

Creon

And this one in a moment!

Oedipus

Ah, friends! What will you do? Will you betray me?
Are you not going to drive this thief away?

Chorus
  Go, stranger! Off with you! You have no right
  To do what you are doing, or what you have done!   825

Creon (to Guards)
  You there: it would be well to take her now,
  Whether she wants to go with you or not.

                              (*Two Guards approach Antigone.*)

Antigone
  Oh, God, where shall I run? What help is there
  From gods or men?

Chorus
                          What are you doing, stranger?

Creon
  I will not touch this man; only her who is mine.   830

Oedipus
  O masters of this land!

Chorus
                          This is unjust!

Creon
  No, just!

Chorus
          Why so?

Creon
                  I take what belongs to me!

Oedipus
  O Athens!

                          (*The Guards pinion Antigone's arms.*)

Chorus
  What are you doing, stranger? Will you
  Let her go? Must we have a test of strength?   835

Creon
  Hold off!

Chorus
                          Not while you persist in doing this!

Creon
　　Your city will have war if you hurt me!

Oedipus
　　Did I not proclaim this?

Chorus (*to Guards*)
　　　　　　　　　　　Take your hands
　　Off the child at once!

Creon
　　　　　　　　　　What you cannot enforce,
　　Do not command!

Chorus
　　I tell you, let go!

Creon
　　　　　　　　　And I tell you—on your way!　　　　840

　　　　　　(*The Guards pull Antigone toward the right.*)

Chorus
　　Help! Here, men of Colonus! Help! Help!
　　The city, my city, is pillaged!
　　Hurry! Help, ho!

Antigone
　　They drag me away. How wretched! O friends, friends!

Oedipus (*groping*)
　　Where are you, child?

Antigone
　　　　　　　　　They have overpowered me!　　　　845

Oedipus
　　Give me your hands, little one!

Antigone
　　　　　　　　　I cannot do it!

Creon (*to Guards*)
　　Will you get on with her?

　　　　　　　　　　　　(*They go out, right.*)

Oedipus
　　　　　　　God help me now!

Creon

    With these two sticks at any rate you'll never
    Guide yourself again! But since you wish
    To conquer your own people—by whose command,   850
    Though I am royal, I have performed this act—
    Go on and conquer! Later, I think, you'll learn
    That now as before you have done yourself no good
    By gratifying your temper against your friends!
    Anger has always been your greatest sin!   855

Chorus (approaching Creon)

    Control yourself, stranger!

Creon

    Don't touch me, I say!

Chorus

    I'll not release you! Those two girls were stolen!

Creon

    By God, I'll have more booty in a moment
    To bring my city! I'll not stop with them!

Chorus

    Now what are you about?

Creon

                 I'll take him, too!   860

Chorus

    A terrible thing to say!

Creon

                 It will be done!

Chorus

    Not if the ruler of our land can help it!

Oedipus

    Voice of shamelessness! Will you touch me?

Creon

    Silence, I say!

Oedipus
                              No! May the powers here
Not make me silent until I say this curse: 865
You scoundrel, who have cruelly taken her
Who served my naked eyepits as their eyes!
On you and yours forever may the sun god,
Watcher of all the world, confer such days
As I have had, and such an age as mine!   870

Creon
Do you see this, citizens of this country?

Oedipus
They see both me and you; and they see also
That when I am hurt I have only words to avenge it!

Creon
I'll not stand for it longer! Alone as I am,
And slow with age, I'll try my strength to take him!   875

                    (*Creon goes slowly toward Oedipus.*)
Oedipus
Ah!

Chorus
                              You are a bold man, friend,
If you think you can do this!

Creon
                              I do think so!
Chorus
If you could do it, our city would be finished!

Creon
In a just cause the weak will beat the strong!   880

Oedipus
You hear his talk?

Chorus
                              By Zeus, he shall not do it!
Creon
Zeus may determine that, but you will not.

Chorus

    Is this not criminal!

Creon (laying hold of Oedipus)

    If so, you'll bear it!

Chorus

    Ho, everyone! Captains, ho!

    Hurry 'up! Come on the run!   885

    They are well on their way by now!

                      (Theseus enters, left, with armed men.)

Theseus

    Why do you shout? What is the matter here?

    Of what are you afraid?

    You have interrupted me as I was sacrificing

    To the great god of the sea, Colonus's patron.

    Tell me everything, so I may know;

    I do not care to make such haste for nothing.   890

Oedipus

    O dearest friend—I recognize your voice—

    A despicable thing has just been done to me!

Theseus

    What is it? Who is the man who did it? Tell me.

Oedipus

    This Creon has had my daughters bound and stolen.   895

Theseus

    What's that you say?

Oedipus

                  Yes; now you know my loss.

Theseus (to his men)

    One of you go on the double

    To the altar place and rouse the people there;

    Make them leave the sacrifice at once

    And run full speed, both foot and cavalry

    As hard as they can gallop, for the place   900

    Where the two highways come together.

The girls must not be permitted to pass there,
Or I will be a laughing-stock to this fellow,
As if I were a man to be handled roughly!
Go on, do as I tell you! Quick!

(Exit Soldier, left.)

This fellow—
If I should act in anger, as he deserves,   905
I wouldn't let him go without chastisement;
But he shall be subject to the sort of laws
He has himself imported here.—

(To Creon)

You: you shall never leave this land of Attica
Until you produce those girls here in my presence;   910
For your behavior is an affront to me,
A shame to your own people and your nation.

You come to a city-state that practices justice,
A state that rules by law, and by law only;
And yet you cast aside her authority,   915
Take what you please, and worse, by violence,
As if you thought there were no men among us,
Or only slaves; and as if I were nobody.

I doubt that Thebes is responsible for you:
She has no propensity for breeding rascals.   920
And Thebes would not applaud you if she knew
You tried to trick me and to rob the gods
By dragging helpless people from their sanctuary!

Were I a visitor in your country—
No matter how immaculate my claims—   925
Without consent from him who ruled the land,
Whoever he might be, I'd take nothing.
I think I have some notion of the conduct
Proper to one who visits a friendly city.
You bring disgrace upon an honorable
Land—your own land, too; a long life   930
Seems to have left you witless as you are old.

I said it once and say it now again:
Someone had better bring those girls here quickly,
Unless you wish to prolong your stay with us
Under close guard, and not much liking it.   935
This is not just a speech; I mean it, friend.

Chorus

Now do you see where you stand? Thebes is just,
But you are adjudged to have acted wickedly.

Creon

It was not that I thought this state unmanly,
Son of Aegeus; nor ill-governed, either;   940
Rather I did this thing in the opinion
That no one here would love my citizens
So tenderly as to keep them against my will . . .
And surely, I thought, no one would give welcome
To an unholy man, a parricide,   945
A man with whom his mother had been found!
Such at least was my estimate of the wisdom
Native to the Areopagus; I thought
Athens was not a home for such exiles.
In that belief I considered him my prize.   950
Even so, I'd not have touched him had he not
Called down curses on my race and me;
That was an injury that deserved reprisal.
There is no old age for a man's anger,
Only death; the dead cannot be hurt.   955

You'll do whatever you wish in this affair,
For even though my case is right and just,
I am weak, without support. Nevertheless,
Old as I am, I'll try to hold you answerable.

Oedipus

O arrogance unashamed! Whose age do you   960
Think you are insulting, mine or yours?
The bloody deaths, the incest, the calamities
You speak so glibly of: I suffered them,

By fate, against my will! It was God's pleasure,
And perhaps our race had angered him long ago. 965
In me myself you could not find such evil
As would have made me sin against my own.
And tell me this: if there were prophecies
Repeated by the oracles of the gods,
That father's death should come through his own son, 970
How could you justly blame it upon me?
On me, who was yet unborn, yet unconceived,
Not yet existent for my father and mother?
If then I came into the world—as I did come—
In wretchedness, and met my father in fight, 975
And knocked him down, not knowing that I killed him
Nor whom I killed—again, how could you find
Guilt in that unmeditated act?
As for my mother—damn you, you have no shame,
Though you are her own brother, in forcing me 980
To speak of that unspeakable marriage;
But I shall speak, I'll not be silent now
After you've let your foul talk go so far!
Yes, she gave me birth—incredible fate!—
But neither of us knew the truth; and she
Bore my children also—and then her shame.
But one thing I do know: you are content 985
To slander her as well as me for that;
While I would not have married her willingly
Nor willingly would I ever speak of it.

No: I shall not be judged an evil man,
Neither in that marriage nor in that death
Which you forever charge me with so bitterly.— 990
Just answer me one thing:
If someone tried to kill you here and now,
You righteous gentleman, what would you do,
Inquire first if the stranger was your father?
Or would you not first try to defend yourself?

I think that since you like to be alive   995
You'd treat him as the threat required; not
Look around for assurance that you were right.
Well, that was the sort of danger I was in,
Forced into it by the gods. My father's soul,
Were it on earth, I know would bear me out.

You, however, being a knave—and since you   1000
Think it fair to say anything you choose,
And speak of what should not be spoken of—
Accuse me of all this before these people.
You also think it clever to flatter Theseus,
And Athens—her exemplary government;
But in your flattery you have forgotten this: 1005
If any country comprehends the honors
Due to the gods, this country knows them best;
Yet you would steal me from Athens in my age
And in my time of prayer; indeed, you seized me,
And you have taken and carried off my daughters.

Now for that profanation I make my prayer,   1010
Calling on the divinities of the grove
That they shall give me aid and fight for me;
So you may know what men defend this town.

Chorus
My lord, our friend is worthy; he has had
Disastrous fortune; yet he deserves our comfort.   1015

Theseus
Enough of speeches. While the perpetrators
Flee, we who were injured loiter here.

Creon
What will you have me do?—since I am worthless.

Theseus
You lead us on the way. You can be my escort.
If you are holding the children in this neighborhood   1020
You yourself will uncover them to me.

If your retainers have taken them in flight,
The chase is not ours; others are after them.
And they will never have cause to thank their gods
For getting free out of this country.
All right. Move on. And remember that the captor   1025
Is now the captive; the hunter is in the snare.
What was won by stealth will not be kept.

In this you'll not have others to assist you;
And I know well you had them, for you'd never
Dare to go so far in your insolence   1030
Were you without sufficient accomplices.
You must have had a reason for your confidence,
And I must reckon with it. The whole city
Must not seem overpowered by one man.
Do you understand at all? Or do you think
That what I say is still without importance?   1035

Creon
    To what you say I make no objection here.
    At home we, too, shall determine what to do.

Theseus
    If you must threaten, do so on the way.
    Oedipus, you stay here, and rest assured
    That unless I perish first I'll not draw breath   1040
    Until I put your children in your hands.

Oedipus
    Bless you for your noble heart, Theseus!
    And good luck to you in what you do for us!

        (*Two Soldiers take Creon by the arms and march him out,
                right, followed by Theseus and the rest of his men.
                    The Chorus follows a short way and stands
                            gazing after them.*)

CHORAL POEM
Chorus
    Ah, God, to be where the pillagers make stand!
    To hear the shout and brazen sound of war!   1045

Or maybe on Apollo's sacred strand,
Or by that torchlit Eleusinian shore

Where pilgrims come, whose lips the golden key   1050
Of sweet-voiced ministers has rendered still,
To cherish there with grave Persephone
Consummate rest from death and mortal ill;

For even to those shades the warrior king   1055
Will press the fighting on—until he take
The virgin sisters from the foemen's ring,
Within his country, for his country's sake!

It may be they will get beyond the plain
And reach the snowy mountain's western side,   1060
If their light chariots have the racing rein,
If they have ponies, and if they can ride;

Yet they'll be taken: for the god they fear
Fights for our land, and Theseus sends forth   1065
His breakneck cavalry with all its gear
Flashing like mountain lightning to the north.

These are the riders of Athens, conquered never;
They honor her whose glory all men know,
And honor the god of the sea, who loves forever   1070
The feminine earth that bore him long ago.

> *(A shift of grouping, and the four following stanzas
> taken each by a separate voice.)*

Chorus

Has the fight begun? May it begin!
The presentiment enchants my mind   1075
That they shall soon give in!
And free the daughters of the blind
From hurt by their own kind!

*For God will see some noble thing
Before this day is over.*

Forevisioning the fight, and proud,   1080
Would I could be a soaring dove

And circle the tall cloud;
So might I gaze down from above
On the mêlée I love.

For God will see some noble thing
Before this day is over.

All highest of immortals! Hail,   1085
Great Zeus who see all things below!
Let not our troopers fail;
But give them luck to snare and throw
And bring the quarry low!

And you shall see some noble thing
Before this day is over.

Stern Pallas, hear us! Apollo, hear!   1090
Hunter and sister who give chase
To the swift and dappled deer:
Be our protectors! Lend your grace
To our land and our race!

And you shall see some noble thing
Before this day is over.

> (*There is a long pause, and then the Chorus turns*
> *to Oedipus in joy.*)

SCENE 5

Chorus

O wanderer! You will not say I lied;
I who kept lookout for you!
I see them now—the two girls—here they come
With our armed men around them!

Oedipus

Ah, where? Do you really mean it?

> (*Theseus comes in leading by the hand Antigone and*
> *Ismene, followed by Soldiers.*)

Antigone

Father, father!
I wish some god would give you eyes to see   1100
The noble prince who brings us back to you!

Oedipus

Ah, child! You are really here?

Antigone

Yes, for the strength
Of Theseus and his kind followers saved us.

Oedipus

Come to your father, child, and let me touch you
Whom I had thought never to touch again!   1105

Antigone

It shall be as you ask; I wish it as much as you.

Oedipus

Where are you?

Antigone

We are coming to you together.

Oedipus

My sweet children!

Antigone

To our father, sweet indeed.

Oedipus

My staff and my support!

Antigone

And partners in sorrow.

Oedipus

I have what is dearest to me in the world.   1110
To die, now, would not be so terrible,
Since you are near me.

Press close to me, child,
Be rooted in your father's arms; rest now
From the cruel separation, the going and coming;
And tell me the story as briefly as you can: 1115
A little talk is enough for girls so tired.

Antigone

    Theseus saved us: he is the one to tell you;
    Neither you nor I had much to do with it!

Oedipus

    Dear friend: don't be offended if I continue
    To talk to these two children overlong;   1120
    I had scarce thought they would be seen again!
    Be sure I understand that you alone
    Made this joy possible for me.
    You are the one that saved them, no one else.
    And may the gods give you such destiny
    As I desire for you: and for your country.   1125
    For I have found you truly reverent,
    Decent, and straight in speech: you only
    Of all mankind.
    I know it, and I thank you with these words.
    All that I have I owe to your courtesy;—
    Now give me your right hand, my lord,   1130
    And if it be permitted, let me kiss you. . . .

    What am I saying? How can a wretch like me
    Desire to touch a man who has no stain
    Of evil in him? No, no; I will not do it;
    And neither shall you touch me. The only ones   1135
    Fit to be fellow suffers of mine
    Are those with such experience as I have.
    Receive my salutation where you are.
    And for the rest, be kindly to me still
    As you have been up to now.

Theseus

    That you should talk a long time to your children
    In joy at seeing them—why, that's no wonder!   1140
    Or that you should address them before me—
    There's no offense in that. It is not in words
    That I should wish my life to be distinguished,
    But rather in things done.

Have I not shown that? I was not a liar   1145
In what I swore I'd do for you, old man.
I am here; and I have brought them back
Alive and safe, for all they were threatened with.
As to how I found them, how I took them, why
Brag of it? You will surely learn from them.

However, there is a matter that just now   1150
Came to my attention on my way here—
A trivial thing to speak of, and yet puzzling;
I want your opinion on it.
It is best for a man not to neglect such things.

Oedipus

What is it, son of Aegeus? Tell me,
So I may know on what you desire counsel.   1155

Theseus

They say some man is here who claims to be
A relative of yours, though not of Thebes;
For some reason he has thrown himself in prayer
Before Poseidon's altar, where I was making
Sacrifice before I came.

Oedipus

What is his country? What is he praying for?   1160

Theseus

All I know is this: he asks, they tell me,
A brief interview with you, and nothing more.

Oedipus

What about, I wonder?
It can't be a slight matter, if he is praying.

Theseus

They say he only asks to speak to you
And then to depart safely by the same road.   1165

Oedipus

Who could it be who would come here to pray?

« 163 »

Theseus

 Think: have you any relative in Argos
 Who might desire this favor of you?

Oedipus

      Dear friend!
 Say no more!

Theseus

      What is the matter with you?

Oedipus

 No more!

Theseus

     But: what is the matter? Tell me.   1170

Oedipus

 When I heard "Argos" I knew the petitioner.

Theseus

 And who is he whom I must prepare to dislike?

Oedipus

 A son of mine, my lord, and a hated one.
 Nothing could be more painful than to listen to him.

Theseus

 But why? Is it not possible to listen   1175
 Without doing anything you need not do?
 Why should it annoy you so to hear him?

Oedipus

 My lord, even his voice is hateful to me.
 Don't beat me down; don't make me yield in this!

Theseus

 But now consider if you are not obliged
 To do so by his supplication here:
 Perhaps you have a duty to the god.   1180

Antigone

 Father: listen to me, even if I am young.
 Allow this man to satisfy his conscience
 And give the gods whatever he thinks their due.
 And let our brother come here, for my sake.

Don't be afraid: he will not throw you off   1185
In your resolve, nor speak offensively.
What is the harm in hearing what he says?
If he has ill intentions, he'll betray them.
You sired him; even had he wronged you, father,
And wronged you impiously, still you could not   1190
Rightfully wrong him in return!
Do let him come!
                 Other men have bad sons,
And other men are swift to anger; yet
They will accept advice, they will be swayed
By their friends' pleading, even against their nature.
Reflect, not on the present, but on the past;   1195
Think of your mother's and your father's fate
And what you suffered through them! If you do,
I think you'll see how terrible an end
Terrible wrath may have.
You have, I think, a permanent reminder
In your lost, irrecoverable eyes. . . .   1200
Ah, yield to us! If our request is just,
We need not, surely, be importunate;
And you, to whom I have not yet been hard,
Should not be obdurate with me!

Oedipus

Child, your talk wins you a pleasure
That will be pain for me. If you have set   1205
Your heart on it, so be it.

Only, Theseus: if he is to come here,
Let no one have power over my life!

Theseus

That is the sort of thing I need hear only
Once, not twice, old man. I do not boast,
But you should know your life is safe while mine is.   1210

*(Theseus goes out, left, with his Soldiers, leaving two on
guard. The Chorus turns to address the audience.)*

CHORAL POEM

Chorus

Though he has watched a decent age pass by,
A man will sometimes still desire the world.
I swear I see no wisdom in that man.
The endless hours pile up a drift of pain
More unrelieved each day; and as for pleasure,   1215
When he is sunken in excessive age,
You will not see his pleasure anywhere.
The last attendant is the same for all,
Old men and young alike, as in its season   1220
Man's heritage of underworld appears:
There being then no epithalamion,
No music and no dance. Death is the finish.

Not to be born surpasses thought and speech.
The second best is to have seen the light   1225
And then to go back quickly whence we came.
The feathery follies of his youth once over,   1230
What trouble is beyond the range of man?
What heavy burden will he not endure?
Jealousy, faction, quarreling, and battle—
The bloodiness of war, the grief of war.
And in the end he comes to strengthless age,   1235
Abhorred by all men, without company,
Unfriended in that uttermost twilight
Where he must live with every bitter thing.

This is the truth, not for me only,
But for this blind and ruined man.
Think of some shore in the north the   1240
Concussive waves make stream
This way and that in the gales of winter:
It is like that with him:
The wild wrack breaking over him
From head to foot, and coming on forever;
Now from the plunging down of the sun,   1245

Now from the sunrise quarter,
Now from where the noonday gleams,
Now from the night and the north.

> (*Antigone and Ismene have been looking off-stage, left.*
> *Antigone turns.*)

SCENE 6

Antigone

    I think I see the stranger near us now,
    And no men with him, father; but his eyes   1250
    Swollen with weeping as he comes.

> (*Polyneices enters, left.*)

Oedipus

                Who comes?

Antigone

    The one whom we have had so long in mind;
    It is he who stands here; it is Polyneices.

Polyneices

    Ah, now what shall I do? Sisters, shall I
    Weep for my misfortunes or for those   1255
    I see in the old man, my father,
    Whom I have found here in an alien land,
    With you two girls, an outcast for so long,
    And with such garments! The abominable
    Filth grown old with him, rotting his sides!
    And on his sightless face the ragged hair   1260
    Streams in the wind. There's the same quality
    In the food he carries for his thin old belly.
    All this I learn too late.
    And I swear now that I have been villainous   1265
    In not supporting you! You need not wait
    To hear it said by others!
                Only, think:
    Compassion limits even the power of God;
    So may there be a limit for you, father!

For all that has gone wrong may still be healed,
And surely the worst is over!   1270

Why are you silent?
Speak to me, father! Don't turn away from me!
Will you not answer me at all? Will you
Send me away without a word?
                              Not even
Tell me why you are enraged against me?

Daughters of Oedipus, my own sisters,   1275
Try to move your so implacable father;
Do not let him reject me in such contempt!
Make him reply!
                              I am here on pilgrimage. . . .

Antigone

Poor brother: you yourself must tell him why.   1280
As men speak on they may sometimes give pleasure,
Sometimes annoy, or sometimes touch the heart;
And so somehow provide the mute with voices.

Polyneices

I will speak out then; your advice is fair.
First, however, I must claim the help   1285
Of that same god, Poseidon, from whose altars
The governor of this land has lifted me
And sent me here, giving me leave to speak
And to await response, and a safe passage.
These are the favors I desire from you,
Stranger, and from my sisters and my father.   1290

And now, father, I will tell you why I came.
I am a fugitive, driven from my country,
Because I thought fit, as the eldest born,
To take my seat upon your sovereign throne.
For that, Eteocles, the younger of us,   1295
Banished me—but not by a decision
In argument or ability or arms;
Merely because he won the city over.

Of this I believe the Furies that pursue you
Were indeed the cause: and so I hear   1300
From clairvoyants whom I afterwards consulted. . . .

Then, when I went into the Dorian land,
I took Adrastus as my father-in-law,
And bound to me by oath whatever men
Were known as leaders or as fighters there;
My purpose being to form an expedition
Of seven troops of spearmen against Thebes.—   1305
With which enlistment may I die for justice
Or else expel the men who exiled me!

So it is. Then why should I come here now?
Father, my prayers must be made to you!
Mine and those of all who fight with me!   1310
Their seven columns under seven captains
Even now complete the encirclement of Thebes:
Men like Amphiareus, the hard spear thrower,
Expert in spears and in the ways of eagles;
Second is Tydeus, the Aetolian,   1315
Son of Oeneus; third is Eteoclus,
Born in Argos; fourth is Hippomedon
(His father, Talaus, sent him); Capaneus,
The fifth, has sworn he'll raze the town of Thebes
With fire-brands; and sixth is Parthenopaeus,   1320
An Arcadian who roused himself to war—
Son of that virgin famous in the old time
Who long years afterward conceived and bore him—
Parthenopaeus, Atalanta's son.
And it is I, your son—or if I am not
Truly your son, since evil fathered me,
At least I am called your son—it is I who lead
The fearless troops of Argos against Thebes.   1325

Now in the name of these two children, father,
And for your own soul's sake, we all implore
And beg you to give up your heavy wrath

Against me! I go forth to punish him,
The brother who robbed me of my fatherland!   1330
If we can put any trust in oracles,
They say that those you bless shall come to power.

Now by the gods and fountains of our people,
I pray you, listen and comply! Are we not beggars
Both of us, and exiles, you and I?   1335
We live by paying court to other men;
The same fate follows us.
But as for him—how insupportable!—
He lords it in our house, luxuriates there,
Laughs at us both!

If you will stand by me in my resolve,
I'll waste no time or trouble whipping him;   1340
And then I'll re-establish you at home,
And settle there myself, and throw him out.
If your will is the same as mine, it's possible
To promise this. If not, I can't be saved.   1345

Chorus

For the sake of the one who sent him, Oedipus,
Speak to this man before you send him back.

Oedipus

Yes, gentlemen: but were it not Theseus,
The sovereign of your land, who sent him here,   1350
Thinking it right that he should have an answer,
You never would have heard a sound from me.

Well: he has asked, and he shall hear from me
A kind of answer that will not overjoy him.
You scoundrel!
                    When it was you who held
Throne and authority—as your brother now   1355
Holds them in Thebes—you drove me into exile:
Me, your own father: made me a homeless man,
Insuring me these rags you blubber over

When you behold them now—now that you, too,
Have fallen on evil days and are in exile.

Weeping is no good now. However long   1360
My life may last, I have to see it through;
But I regard you as a murderer!
For you reduced me to this misery,
You made me an alien. Because of you
I have begged my daily bread from other men.
If I had not these children to sustain me,   1365
I might have lived or died for all your interest.
But they have saved me, they are my support,
And are not girls, but men, in faithfulness.
As for you two, you are no sons of mine!

And so it is that there are eyes that watch you   1370
Even now; though not as they shall watch
If those troops are in fact marching on Thebes.
You cannot take that city. You'll go down
All bloody, and your brother, too.
                            For I
Have placed that curse upon you before this,   1375
And now I invoke that curse to fight for me,
That you may see a reason to respect
Your parents, though your birth was as it was;
And though I am blind, not to dishonor me.
These girls did not.

And so your supplication and your throne   1380
Are overmastered surely,—if accepted
Justice still has place in the laws of God.
Now go! For I abominate and disown you!
You utter scoundrel! Go with the malediction
I here pronounce for you: that you shall never   1385
Master your native land by force of arms,
Nor ever see your home again in Argos,
The land below the hills; but you shall die
By your own brother's hand, and you shall kill

The brother who banished you. For this I pray.
And I cry out to the hated underworld   1390
That it may take you home; cry out to those
Powers indwelling here; and to that Power
Of furious War that filled your hearts with hate!

Now you have heard me. Go: tell it to Thebes,
Tell all the Thebans; tell your faithful fighting
Friends what sort of honors   1395
Oedipus has divided among his sons!

Chorus
  Polyneices, your coming here has given me
  No joy at all. Now go away at once.

Polyneices
  Ah, what a journey! What a failure!
  My poor companions! See the finish now   1400
  Of all we marched from Argos for! See me . . .
  For I can neither speak of this to anyone
  Among my friends, nor lead them back again;
  I must go silently to meet this doom.

  O sisters—daughters of his, sisters of mine!   1405
  You heard the hard curse of our father:
  For God's sweet sake, if father's curse comes true,
  And if you find some way to return home,
  Do not, at least, dishonor me in death!
  But give me a grave and what will quiet me.   1410
  Then you shall have, besides the praise he now
  Gives you for serving him, an equal praise
  For offices you shall have paid my ghost.

Antigone
  Polyneices, I beseech you, listen to me!

Polyneices
  Dearest—what is it? Tell me, Antigone.   1415

Antigone

    Withdraw your troops to Argos as soon as you can.
    Do not go to your own death and your city's!

Polyneices

    But that is impossible. How could I command
    That army, even backward, once I faltered?

Antigone

    Now why, boy, must your anger rise again?   1420
    What is the good of laying waste your homeland?

Polyneices

    It is shameful to run; and it is also shameful
    To be a laughing-stock to a younger brother.

Antigone

    But see how you fulfill his prophecies!
    Did he not cry that you should kill each other?   1425

Polyneices

    He wishes that. But I cannot give way.

Antigone

    Ah, I am desolate! But who will dare
    Go with you, after hearing the prophecies?

Polyneices

    I'll not report this trifle. A good commander
    Tells what is encouraging, not what is not.   1430

Antigone

    Then you have made up your mind to this, my brother?

Polyneices

    Yes. And do not try to hold me back.
    The dark road is before me; I must take it,
    Doomed by my father and his avenging Furies.
    God bless you if you do what I have asked: 1435
    It is only in death that you can help me now.
    Now let me go. Good-bye! You will not ever
    Look in my eyes again.

Antigone

You break my heart!

Polyneices
  Do not grieve for me.

Antigone

Who would not grieve for you,
  Sweet brother! You go with open eyes to death!   1440

Polyneices
  Death, if that must be.

Antigone

No! Do as I ask!

Polyneices
  You ask the impossible.

Antigone

Then I am lost,
  If I must be deprived of you!

Polyneices

All that
  Rests with the powers that are over us,—
  Whether it must be so or otherwise.
  You two—I pray no evil comes to you,   1445
  For all men know you merit no more pain.

(*Polyneices goes out, left. There is a dead silence;
                  then the Chorus meditates.*)

CHORAL POEM AND DIALOGUE

Chorus
  So in this new event we see
  New forms of terror working through the blind,
  Or else inscrutable destiny.   1450
  I am not one to say "This is in vain"
  Of anything allotted to mankind.
  Though some must fall, or fall to rise again,
  Time watches all things steadily—   1455
                  (*A terrific peal of thunder.*)

Ah, Zeus! Heaven's height has cracked!

(*Thunder and lightning.*)

Oedipus

O my child, my child! Could someone here—
Could someone bring the hero, Theseus?

Antigone

Father, what is your reason for calling him?

Oedipus

God's beating thunder, any moment now,   1460
Will clap me underground: send for him quickly!

(*Thunder and lightning.*)

Chorus

Hear it cascading down the air!
The god-thrown, the gigantic, holy sound!
Terror crawls to the tips of my hair!   1465
My heart shakes!
        There the lightning flames again!
What heavenly marvel is it bringing 'round?
I fear it, for it never comes in vain,
But for man's luck or his despair. . . .   1470

(*Another terrific peal.*)

Ah, Zeus! Majestic heaven!

Oedipus

My children, the appointed end has come;
I can no longer turn away from it.

Antigone

How do you know? What is the sign that tells you?

Oedipus

I know it clearly now. Let someone quickly   1475
Send for the king and bring him here to me!

(*Thunder and lightning.*)

Chorus

Hear the wild thunder fall!
Towering Nature is transfixed!

Be merciful, great spirit, if you run   1480
This sword of darkness through our mother land;
Come not for our confusion,
And deal no blows to me,
Though your tireless Furies stand
By him whom I have looked upon.
Great Zeus, I make my prayer to thee!   1485

Oedipus

Is the king near by? Will he come in time
To find me still alive, my mind still clear?

Antigone

Tell me what it is you have in mind!

Oedipus

To give him now, in return for his great kindness,
The blessing that I promised I would give.   1490

                                                (Thunder.)

Chorus

O noble son, return!
No matter if you still descend
In the deep fastness of the sea god's grove,
To make pure offering at his altar fire:
Come back quickly, for God's love!   1495
Receive from this strange man
Whatever may be his heart's desire
That you and I and Athens are worthy of.
My lord, come quickly as you can!

                *(The thunder continues, until it stops abruptly with
                            the entrance of Theseus, left.)*

                            SCENE 7
Theseus

Now why do you all together   1500
Set up this shout once more?
I see it comes from you, as from our friend.
Is it a lightning bolt from God? a squall

Of rattling hail? Those are familiar things
When such a tempest rages over heaven.

Oedipus

My lord, I longed for you to come! This is   1505
God's work, your lucky coming.

Theseus

Now, what new
Circumstance has arisen, son of Laius?

Oedipus

My life sinks in the scale: I would not die
Without fulfilling what I promised Athens.

Theseus

What proof have you that your hour has come?   1510

Oedipus

The great, incessant thunder and continuous
Flashes of lightning from the hand of God.   1515

Theseus

I believe you. I have seen you prophesy
Many things, none falsely. What must be done?

Oedipus

I shall disclose to you, O son of Aegeus,
What is appointed for you and for your city:
A thing that age will never wear away.
Presently now, without a soul to guide me,   1520
I'll lead you to the place where I must die;
But you must never tell it to any man,
Not even the neighborhood in which it lies.
If you obey, this will count more for you
Than many shields and many neighbors' spears.   1525
These things are mysteries, not to be explained;
But you will understand when you come there
Alone. Alone, because I cannot disclose it
To any of your men or to my children,
Much as I love and cherish them. But you

Keep it secret always, and when you come   1530
To the end of life, then you must hand it on
To your most cherished son, and he in turn
Must teach it to his heir, and so forever.
That way you shall forever hold this city
Safe from the men of Thebes, the dragon's sons.

For every nation that lives peaceably,
There will be many others to grow hard
And push their arrogance to extremes: the gods   1535
Attend to these things slowly. But they attend
To those who put off God and turn to madness!
You have no mind for that, child of Aegeus;
Indeed, you know already all that I teach.

Let us proceed then to that place   1540
And hesitate no longer; I am driven
By an insistent voice that comes from God.
Children, follow me this way: see, now,
I have become your guide, as you were mine!
Come: do not touch me: let me alone discover
The holy and funereal ground where I   1545
Must take this fated earth to be my shroud.

This way, O come! The angel of the dead,
Hermes, and veiled Persephone lead me on!

        (He leads them, firmly and slowly, to the left.)
O sunlight of no light! Once you were mine!
This is the last my flesh will feel of you;   1550
For now I go to shade my ending day
In the dark underworld. Most cherished friend!
I pray that you and this your land and all
Your people may be blessed: remember me,
Be mindful of my death, and be
Fortunate in all the time to come!   1555

*(Oedipus goes out, followed by his children and by Theseus
with his Soldiers. The Chorus lifts its arms to pray.)*

CHORAL POEM

Chorus

If I may dare to adore that Lady
The living never see,
And pray to the master of spirits plunged in night,
Who of vast Hell has sovereignty;
Let not our friend go down in grief and weariness   1560
To that all-shrouding cold,
The dead men's plain, the house that has no light.
Because his sufferings were great, unmerited and untold,   1565
Let some just god relieve him from distress!

O powers under the earth, and tameless
Beast in the passage way,   1570
Rumbler prone at the gate of the strange hosts,
Their guard forever, the legends say:
I pray you, even Death, offspring of Earth and Hell,
To let the descent be clear   1575
As Oedipus goes down among the ghosts
On those dim fields of underground that all men living fear.
Eternal sleep, let Oedipus sleep well!

(A long pause. A Messenger comes in, left.)

SCENE 8

Messenger

Citizens, the briefest way to tell you
Would be to say that Oedipus is no more;   1580
But what has happened cannot be told so simply—
It was no simple thing.

Chorus

      He is gone, poor man?

Messenger

You may be sure that he has left this world.

Chorus

By God's mercy, was his death a painless one?   1585

Messenger

That is the thing that seems so marvelous.

You know, for you were witnesses, how he
Left this place with no friend leading him,
Acting, himself, as guide for all of us.
Well, when he came to the steep place in the road,   1590
The embankment there, secured with steps of brass,
He stopped in one of the many branching paths.

This was not far from the stone bowl that marks
Theseus' and Pirithous' covenant.

Half-way between that place of stone
With its hollow pear tree, and the marble tomb,   1595
He sat down and undid his filthy garments;
Then he called his daughters and commanded
That they should bring him water from a fountain
For bathing and libation to the dead.
From there they could see the hill of Demeter,   1600
Freshener of all things: so they ascended it
And soon came back with water for their father;
Then helped him properly to bathe and dress.

When everything was finished to his pleasure,
And no command of his remained undone,   1605
Then the earth groaned with thunder from the god below;
And as they heard the sound, the girls shuddered,
And dropped to their father's knees, and began wailing,
Beating their breasts and weeping as if heartbroken.
And hearing them cry out so bitterly,   1610
He put his arms around them, and said to them:

"Children, this day your father is gone from you.
All that was mine is gone. You shall no longer
Bear the burden of taking care of me—
I know it was hard, my children.—And yet one word   1615
Makes all those difficulties disappear:
That word is love. You never shall have more

From any man than you have had from me.
And now you must spend the rest of life without me."

That was the way of it. They clung together   1620
And wept, all three. But when they finally stopped,
And no more sobs were heard, then there was
Silence, and in the silence suddenly
A voice cried out to him—of such a kind
It made our hair stand up in panic fear: 1625
Again and again the call came from the god:
"Oedipus! Oedipus! Why are we waiting?
You delay too long; you delay too long to go!"

Then, knowing himself summoned by the spirit,
He asked that the lord Theseus come to him;   1630
And when he had come, said: "O beloved one,
Give your right hand now as a binding pledge
To my two daughters; children, give him your hands.
Promise that you will never willingly
Betray them, but will carry out in kindness
Whatever is best for them in the days to come."   1635

And Theseus swore to do it for his friend,
With such restraint as fits a noble king.
And when he had done so, Oedipus at once
Laid his blind hands upon his daughters, saying:
"Children, you must show your nobility,   1640
And have the courage now to leave this spot.
You must not wish to see what is forbidden,
Or hear what may not afterward be told.
But go—go quickly. Only the lord Theseus
May stay to see the thing that now begins."

This much every one of us heard him say,   1645
And then we came away with the sobbing girls.
But after a little while as we withdrew
We turned around—and nowhere saw that man,
But only the king, his hands before his face,   1650

Shading his eyes as if from something awful,
Fearful and unendurable to see.
Then very quickly we saw him do reverence
To Earth and to the powers of the air,
With one address to both.

                        But in what manner   1655
Oedipus perished, no one of mortal men
Could tell but Theseus. It was not lightning,
Bearing its fire from God, that took him off;
No hurricane was blowing.   1660
But some attendant from the train of Heaven
Came for him; or else the underworld
Opened in love the unlit door of earth.
For he was taken without lamentation,
Illness or suffering; indeed his end
Was wonderful if mortal's ever was.   1665

Should someone think I speak intemperately,
I make no apology to him who thinks so.

Chorus
But where are his children and the others with them?

Messenger
They are not far away; the sound of weeping
Should tell you now that they are coming here.

            (Antigone and Ismene enter together.)

CHORAL DIALOGUE
Antigone
Now we may weep, indeed.   1670
Now, if ever, we may cry
In bitter grief against our fate,
Our heritage still unappeased.
In other days we stood up under it,
Endured it for his sake,
The unrelenting horror. Now the finish   1675
Comes, and we know only

In all that we have seen and done
Bewildering mystery.

Chorus

What happened?

Antigone

     We can only guess, my friends.

Chorus

He has gone?

Antigone

    He has; as one could wish him to.
Why not? It was not war
Nor the deep sea that overtook him,   1680
But something invisible and strange
Caught him up—or down—
Into a space unseen.
But we are lost. A deathly
Night is ahead of us.
For how, in some far country wandering,   1685
Or on the lifting seas,
Shall we eke out our lives?

Ismene

I cannot guess. But as for me
I wish that charnel Hell would take me   1690
In one death with our father.
This is such desolation
I cannot go on living.

Chorus

Most admirable sisters:
Whatever God has brought about
Is to be borne with courage.
You must not feed the flames of grief.   1695
No blame can come to you.

Antigone

One may long for the past
Though at the time indeed it seemed

Nothing but wretchedness and evil.
Life was not sweet, yet I found it so
When I could put my arms around my father.
O father! O my dear! 1700
Now you are shrouded in eternal darkness,
Even in that absence
You shall not lack our love,
Mine and my sister's love.

Chorus
He lived his life.

Antigone
He did as he had wished!

Chorus
What do you mean?

Antigone
In this land among strangers 1705
He died where he chose to die.
He has his eternal bed well shaded,
And in his death is not unmourned.
My eyes are blind with tears
From crying for you, father. 1710
The terror and the loss
Cannot be quieted.
I know you wished to die in a strange country,
Yet your death was so lonely!
Why could I not be with you?

Ismene
O pity! What is left for me? 1715
What destiny awaits us both
Now we have lost our father?

Chorus
Dear children, remember 1720
That his last hour was free and blessed.
So make an end of grieving!

Is anyone in all the world
Safe from unhappiness?

Antigone
Let us run back there!

Ismene
                    Why, what shall we do?

Antigone
I am carried away with longing—

Ismene
                              For what,—tell me!   1725

Antigone
To see the resting place in the earth—

Ismene
                                    Of whom?

Antigone
Oh, father's! O dear God, I am so unhappy!

Ismene
But that is not permitted. Do you not see?

Antigone
Do not rebuke me!

Ismene
                    —And remember, too—   1730

Antigone
Oh, what?

Ismene
              He had no tomb, there was no one near!

Antigone
Take me there and you can kill me, too!

Ismene
Ah! I am truly lost!
Helpless and so forsaken!   1735
Where shall I go and how shall I live?

Chorus
Don't be afraid, now.

Antigone
                        Yes, but where is a refuge?

Chorus
    A refuge has been found—

Antigone
                            Where do you mean?

Chorus
    A place where you will be unharmed!

Antigone
                                No . . .   1740

Chorus
    What are you thinking?

Antigone
                                I think there is no way
    For me to get home again.

Chorus
                        Do not go home!

Antigone
    My home is in trouble.

Chorus
                        So it has been before.

Antigone
    There was no help for it then: but now it is worse.   1745

Chorus
    A wide and desolate world it is for you.

Antigone
    Great God! What way is there?
    Do the powers that rule our lives
    Still press me on to hope at all?   1750

                        (*Theseus comes in, with attendants.*)
Theseus
    Mourn no more, children. Those to whom
    The night of earth gives benediction
    Should not be mourned. Retribution comes.

Antigone
    Theseus: we fall on our knees to you!

Theseus

>What is it that you desire, children?   1755

Antigone

>We wish to see the place ourselves
>In which our father rests.

Theseus

>   No, no.
>It is not permissible to go there.

Antigone

>My lord and ruler of Athens, why?

Theseus

>Because your father told me, children,   1760
>That no one should go near the spot,
>No mortal man should tell of it,
>Since it is holy, and is his.
>And if I kept this pledge, he said,
>I should preserve my land from its enemies.   1765
>I swore I would, and the god heard me:
>The oathkeeper who keeps track of all.

Antigone

>If this was our father's cherished wish,
>We must be satisfied.
>Send us back, then, to ancient Thebes,   1770
>And we may stop the bloody war
>From coming between our brothers!

Theseus

>I will do that, and whatever else
>I am able to do for your happiness,
>For his sake who has gone just now   1775
>Beneath the earth. I must not fail.

Chorus

>Now let the weeping cease;
>Let no one mourn again.
>These things are in the hands of God.

THE BACCHAE

Translated by William Arrowsmith

INTRODUCTION

Euripides wrote *The Bacchae* in the last years of his life during a self-imposed exile in Macedon. It was produced in Athens after his death, which occurred in 406 B.C., and won a posthumous first prize.

Dionysus himself speaks a most explicit prologue, setting forth the facts of his case, and the action proceeds from this point along clearly drawn lines. The reader needs no summary. But a few comments may help. Dionysus, on stage as a mortal, is a new god fighting for recognition as a god in the city of his birth, which should be the first to recognize him and has rejected him. If he is the acknowledged son of Zeus and Semele, he would be at least heroic; in this case he is divine. If Zeus is not his father, he is a bastard foundling and an impostor. Through madness and slaughter he punishes his doubting kinsmen and is established as a god at the end.

The actual drama is played out as a struggle between two young men, Dionysus and his cousin Pentheus, master of Thebes. Above and beyond the individuals, even the god, is what Dionysus stands for, not wine only, but a new kind of religion. Accepted, it means pious devotion; resisted, it will still force its way in, as madness. The devout Bacchae of the Chorus have accepted; the mad women in the hills have had Bacchism forced on them. Pentheus is defeated by invasion from within, and his integrity has surrendered to the power of Dionysus before he goes to his death. The utterances of the Chorus constantly go beyond the immediate issues of the action, to celebrate a new religious feeling, open to the will of all human beings, barbarians as well as Hellenes, the weak, poor, and unlettered as well as the strong, rich, and wise. These choral odes, the wildest and most original to be found in Euripides, do somewhat to relieve the horrors in a story of vengeance and brutal punishment.

NOTE

The text of this translation is the Oxford text of Gilbert Murray, supplemented by the brilliant commentary of E. R. Dodds.

CHARACTERS

Dionysus (*also called Bromius, Evius, and Bacchus*)

Chorus of Asian Bacchae (*followers of Dionysus*)

Teiresias

Cadmus

Pentheus

Attendant

First Messenger

Second Messenger

Agave

Coryphaeus (*chorus leader*)

For Anne and George
ex voto
XAIPETE

THE BACCHAE

Scene: *Before the royal palace at Thebes. On the left is the way to Cithaeron; on the right, to the city. In the center of the orchestra stands, still smoking, the vine-covered tomb of Semele, mother of Dionysus.*

Enter Dionysus. He is of soft, even effeminate, appearance. His face is beardless; he is dressed in a fawn-skin and carries a thyrsus (i.e., a stalk of fennel tipped with ivy leaves). On his head he wears a wreath of ivy, and his long blond curls ripple down over his shoulders. Throughout the play he wears a smiling mask.

Dionysus

I am Dionysus, the son of Zeus,
come back to Thebes, this land where I was born.
My mother was Cadmus' daughter, Semele by name,
midwived by fire, delivered by the lightning's
blast.

And here I stand, a god incognito,
disguised as man, beside the stream of Dirce   5
and the waters of Ismenus. There before the palace
I see my lightning-married mother's grave,
and there upon the ruins of her shattered house
the living fire of Zeus still smolders on
in deathless witness of Hera's violence and rage
against my mother. But Cadmus wins my praise: 10
he has made this tomb a shrine, sacred to my mother.
It was I who screened her grave with the green
of the clustering vine.

Far behind me lie
those golden-rivered lands, Lydia and Phrygia,
where my journeying began. Overland I went,
across the steppes of Persia where the sun strikes hotly
down, through Bactrian fastness and the grim waste   15
of Media. Thence to rich Arabia I came;

and so, along all Asia's swarming littoral
of towered cities where Greeks and foreign nations,
mingling, live, my progress made. There
I taught my dances to the feet of living men,
establishing my mysteries and rites
that I might be revealed on earth for what I am:
a god.
      And thence to Thebes.

                  This city, first   20
in Hellas, now shrills and echoes to my women's cries,
their ecstasy of joy. Here in Thebes
I bound the fawn-skin to the women's flesh and armed
their hands with shafts of ivy. For I have come   25
to refute that slander spoken by my mother's sisters—
those who least had right to slander her.
They said that Dionysus was no son of Zeus,
but Semele had slept beside a man in love
and fathered off her shame on Zeus—a fraud, they sneered,   30
contrived by Cadmus to protect his daughter's name.
They said she lied, and Zeus in anger at that lie
blasted her with lightning.
                Because of that offense
I have stung them with frenzy, hounded them from home
up to the mountains where they wander, crazed of mind,
and compelled to wear my orgies' livery.
Every woman in Thebes—but the women only—   35
I drove from home, mad. There they sit,
rich and poor alike, even the daughters of Cadmus,
beneath the silver firs on the roofless rocks.
Like it or not, this city must learn its lesson:
it lacks initiation in my mysteries;   40
that I shall vindicate my mother Semele
and stand revealed to mortal eyes as the god
she bore to Zeus.
            Cadmus the king has abdicated,
leaving his throne and power to his grandson Pentheus;

who now revolts against divinity, in *me;*   45
thrusts *me* from his offerings; forgets *my* name
in his prayers. Therefore I shall *prove* to him
and every man in Thebes that I am god
indeed. And when my worship is established here,
and all is well, then I shall go my way
and be revealed to other men in other lands.   50
But if the men of Thebes attempt to force
my Bacchae from the mountainside by threat of arms,
I shall marshal my Maenads and take the field.
To these ends I have laid my deity aside
and go disguised as man.

>   (*He wheels and calls offstage.*)

>   On, my women,   55
women who worship me, women whom I led
out of Asia where Tmolus heaves its rampart
over Lydia!
>   On, comrades of my progress here!
Come, and with your native Phrygian drum—
Rhea's drum and mine—pound at the palace doors   60
of Pentheus! Let the city of Thebes behold you,
while I return among Cithaeron's forest glens
where my Bacchae wait and join their whirling dances.

>   (*Exit Dionysus as the Chorus of Asian Bacchae comes
>   dancing in from the right. They are dressed in
>   fawn-skins, crowned with ivy, and carry
>   thyrsi, timbrels, and flutes.*)

Chorus

>   Out of the land of Asia,
>   down from holy Tmolus,   65
>   speeding the service of god,
>   for Bromius we come!
>   Hard are the labors of god;
>   hard, but his service is sweet.
>   Sweet to serve, sweet to cry:
>   *Bacchus!   Evohé!*

—You on the streets!

        —You on the roads!

                —Make way!

—Let every mouth be hushed. Let no ill-omened words   70
  profane your tongues.

              —Make way! Fall back!

                  —Hush.

—For now I raise the old, old hymn to Dionysus.

—Blessèd, blessèd are those who know the mysteries of god.
—Blessèd is he who hallows his life in the worship of god,
  he whom the spirit of god possesseth, who is one
  with those who belong to the holy body of god.   75
—Blessèd are the dancers and those who are purified,
  who dance on the hill in the holy dance of god.
—Blessèd are they who keep the rite of Cybele the Mother.
—Blessèd are the thyrsus-bearers, those who wield in their hands
  the holy wand of god.   80
—Blessèd are those who wear the crown of the ivy of god.
—Blessèd, blessèd are they: Dionysus is their god!

—On, Bacchae, on, you Bacchae,
  bear your god in triumph home!
  Bear on the god, son of god,
  escort your Dionysus home!   85
  Bear him down from Phrygian hill,
  attend him through the streets of Hellas!

—So his mother bore him once
  in labor bitter; lightning-struck,
  forced by fire that flared from Zeus,   90
  consumed, she died, untimely torn,
  in childbed dead by blow of light!
  Of light the son was born!

—Zeus it was who saved his son;   95
  with speed outrunning mortal eye,

bore him to a private place,
bound the boy with clasps of gold;
in his thigh as in a womb,   #4
concealed his son from Hera's eyes.

—And when the weaving Fates fulfilled the time,   100
the bull-horned god was born of Zeus. In joy
he crowned his son, set serpents on his head—
wherefrom, in piety, descends to us
the Maenad's writhing crown, her *chevelure* of snakes.

—O Thebes, nurse of Semele,   105
crown your hair with ivy!
Grow green with bryony!
Redden with berries! O city,
with boughs of oak and fir,   110
come dance the dance of god!
Fringe your skins of dappled fawn
with tufts of twisted wool!
Handle with holy care
the violent wand of god!
And let the dance begin!
He is Bromius who runs   115
to the mountain!
             to the mountain!
where the throng of women waits,
driven from shuttle and loom,
possessed by Dionysus!

—And I praise the holies of Crete,   120
the caves of the dancing Curetes,
there where Zeus was born,
where helmed in triple tier
around the primal drum
the Corybantes danced. They,   125
they were the first of all
whose whirling feet kept time

to the strict beat of the taut hide
and the squeal of the wailing flute.
Then from them to Rhea's hands
the holy drum was handed down;
but, stolen by the raving Satyrs,   130
fell at last to me and now
accompanies the dance
which every other year
celebrates your name:
    Dionysus!

—He is sweet upon the mountains. He drops to the earth   135
    from the running packs.
He wears the holy fawn-skin. He hunts the wild goat
    and kills it.
He delights in the raw flesh.
He runs to the mountains of Phrygia, to the mountains
    of Lydia he runs!   140
He is Bromius who leads us! *Evohé!*

—With milk the earth flows! It flows with wine!
It runs with the nectar of bees!

—Like frankincense in its fragrance
is the blaze of the torch he bears.   145
Flames float out from his trailing wand
    as he runs, as he dances,
    kindling the stragglers,
    spurring with cries,
and his long curls stream to the wind!   150

—And he cries, as they cry, *Evohé!*—
    On, Bacchae!
    On, Bacchae!
Follow, glory of golden Tmolus,
    hymning god   155
    with a rumble of drums,

with a cry, *Evohé!* to the Evian god,
with a cry of Phrygian cries,
when the holy flute like honey plays   160
the sacred song of those who go
to the mountain!
                            to the mountain!   165

—Then, in ecstasy, like a colt by its grazing mother,
the Bacchante runs with flying feet, she leaps!

> (*The Chorus remains grouped in two semicircles about the
> orchestra as Teiresias makes his entrance. He is in-
> congruously dressed in the bacchant's fawn-skin
> and is crowned with ivy. Old and blind,
> he uses his thyrsus to tap his way.*)

Teiresias

Ho there, who keeps the gates?
                            Summon Cadmus—   170
Cadmus, Agenor's son, the stranger from Sidon
who built the towers of our Thebes.
                            Go, someone.
Say Teiresias wants him. He will know what errand
brings me, that agreement, age with age, we made   175
to deck our wands, to dress in skins of fawn
and crown our heads with ivy.

> (*Enter Cadmus from the palace. Dressed in Dionysiac
> costume and bent almost double with age, he is an
> incongruous and pathetic figure.*)

Cadmus
                            My old friend,
I knew it must be you when I heard your summons.
For there's a wisdom in his voice that makes
the man of wisdom known.
                            But here I am,
dressed in the costume of the god, prepared to go.   180
Insofar as we are able, Teiresias, we must

do honor to this god, for he was born
my daughter's son, who has been revealed to men,
the god, Dionysus.

      Where shall we go, where
shall we tread the dance, tossing our white heads
in the dances of god?

       Expound to me, Teiresias.   185
For in such matters you are wise.

         Surely
I could dance night and day, untiringly
beating the earth with my thyrsus! And how sweet it is
to forget my old age.

Teiresias

      It is the same with me.
I too feel young, young enough to dance.   190

Cadmus

  Good. Shall we take our chariots to the mountain?

Teiresias

  Walking would be better. It shows more honor
to the god.

Cadmus

    So be it. I shall lead, my old age
conducting yours.

Teiresias

    The god will guide us there
with no effort on our part.

Cadmus

      Are we the only men   195
who will dance for Bacchus?

Teiresias

      They are all blind.
Only we can see.

Cadmus

But we delay too long.
Here, take my arm.

Teiresias

Link my hand in yours.

Cadmus

I am a man, nothing more. I do not scoff
at heaven.

Teiresias

We do not trifle with divinity.   200
No, we are the heirs of customs and traditions
hallowed by age and handed down to us
by our fathers. No quibbling logic can topple *them*,
whatever subtleties this clever age invents.
People may say: "Aren't you ashamed? At your age,
going dancing, wreathing your head with ivy?"   205
Well, I am *not* ashamed. Did the god declare
that just the young or just the old should dance?
No, he desires his honor from all mankind.
He wants no one excluded from his worship.

Cadmus

Because you cannot see, Teiresias, let me be   210
interpreter for you this once. Here comes
the man to whom I left my throne, Echion's son,
Pentheus, hastening toward the palace. He seems
excited and disturbed. Yes, listen to him.

> (*Enter Pentheus from the right. He is a young man of
> athletic build, dressed in traditional Greek dress;
> like Dionysus, he is beardless. He enters
> excitedly, talking to the attendants
> who accompany him.*)

Pentheus

I happened to be away, out of the city,   215
but reports reached me of some strange mischief here,

stories of our women leaving home to frisk
in mock ecstasies among the thickets on the mountain,
dancing in honor of the latest divinity,
a certain Dionysus, whoever he may be!   220
In their midst stand bowls brimming with wine.
And then, one by one, the women wander off
to hidden nooks where they serve the lusts of men.
Priestesses of Bacchus they claim they are,
but it's really Aphrodite they adore.   225
I have captured some of them; my jailers
have locked them away in the safety of our prison.
Those who run at large shall be hunted down
out of the mountains like the animals they are—
yes, my own mother Agave, and Ino
and Autonoë, the mother of Actaeon.   230
In no time at all I shall have them trapped
in iron nets and stop this obscene disorder.

    I am also told a foreigner has come to Thebes
from Lydia, one of those charlatan magicians,
with long yellow curls smelling of perfumes,   235
with flushed cheeks and the spells of Aphrodite
in his eyes. His days and nights he spends
with women and girls, dangling before them the joys
of initiation in his mysteries.
But let me bring him underneath that roof
and I'll stop his pounding with his wand and tossing   240
his head. By god, I'll have his head cut off!
And *this* is the man who claims that Dionysus
is a god and was sewn into the thigh of Zeus,
when, in point of fact, that same blast of lightning
consumed him and his mother both for her lie   245
that she had lain with Zeus in love. Whoever
this stranger is, aren't such impostures,
such unruliness, worthy of hanging?

                (For the first time he sees Teiresias and
                   Cadmus in their Dionysiac costumes.)

What!

But this is incredible! Teiresias the seer
tricked out in a dappled fawn-skin!

         And *you*,
you, my own grandfather, playing at the bacchant   250
with a wand!

         Sir, I shrink to see your old age
so foolish. Shake that ivy off, grandfather!
Now drop that wand. Drop it, I say.

              (*He wheels on Teiresias.*)

         Aha,
I see: this is *your* doing, Teiresias.   255
Yes, you want still another god revealed to men
so you can pocket the profits from burnt offerings
and bird-watching. By heaven, only your age
restrains me now from sending you to prison
with those Bacchic women for importing here to Thebes
these filthy mysteries. When once you see   260
the glint of wine shining at the feasts of women,
then you may be sure the festival is rotten.

Coryphaeus

What blasphemy! Stranger, have you no respect
for heaven? For Cadmus who sowed the dragon teeth?
Will the son of Echion disgrace his house?   265

Teiresias

Give a wise man an honest brief to plead
and his eloquence is no remarkable achievement.
But you are glib; your phrases come rolling out
smoothly on the tongue, as though your words were wise
instead of foolish. The man whose glibness flows
from his conceit of speech declares the thing he is: 270
a worthless and a stupid citizen.

         I tell you,
this god whom you ridicule shall someday have

enormous power and prestige throughout Hellas.
Mankind, young man, possesses two supreme blessings.
First of these is the goddess Demeter, or Earth— 275
whichever name you choose to call her by.
It was she who gave to man his nourishment of grain.
But after her there came the son of Semele,
who matched her present by inventing liquid wine
as his gift to man. For filled with that good gift,
suffering mankind forgets its grief; from it 280
comes sleep; with it oblivion of the troubles
of the day. There is no other medicine
for misery. And when we pour libations
to the gods, we pour the god of wine himself
that through his intercession man may win 285
the favor of heaven.

> You sneer, do you, at that story
that Dionysus was sewed into the thigh of Zeus?
Let me teach you what that really means. When Zeus
rescued from the thunderbolt his infant son,
he brought him to Olympus. Hera, however,
plotted at heart to hurl the child from heaven. 290
Like the god he is, Zeus countered her. Breaking off
a tiny fragment of that ether which surrounds the world,
he molded from it a dummy Dionysus.
This he *showed* to Hera, but with time men garbled
the word and said that Dionysus had been *sewed* 295
into the thigh of Zeus. This was their story,
whereas, in fact, Zeus *showed* the dummy to Hera
and gave it as a hostage for his son.

> Moreover,
this is a god of prophecy. His worshippers,
like madmen, are endowed with mantic powers.
For when the god enters the body of a man 300
he fills him with the breath of prophecy.

> Besides,

he has usurped even the functions of warlike Ares.
Thus, at times, you see an army mustered under arms
stricken with panic before it lifts a spear.
This panic comes from Dionysus.

                        Someday   305
you shall even see him bounding with his torches
among the crags at Delphi, leaping the pastures
that stretch between the peaks, whirling and waving
his thyrsus: great throughout Hellas.

                            Mark my words,
Pentheus. Do not be so certain that power   310
is what matters in the life of man; do not mistake
for wisdom the fantasies of your sick mind.
Welcome the god to Thebes; crown your head;
pour him libations and join his revels.

   Dionysus does not, I admit, *compel* a woman
to be chaste. Always and in every case   315
it is her character and nature that keeps
a woman chaste. But even in the rites of Dionysus,
the chaste woman will not be corrupted.

                           Think:
you are pleased when men stand outside your doors
and the city glorifies the name of Pentheus.   320
And so the god: he too delights in glory.
But Cadmus and I, whom you ridicule, will crown
our heads with ivy and join the dances of the god—
an ancient foolish pair perhaps, but dance
we must. Nothing you have said would make me
change my mind or flout the will of heaven.   325
You are mad, grievously mad, beyond the power
of any drugs to cure, for you are drugged
with madness.

Coryphaeus
                Apollo would approve your words.
Wisely you honor Bromius: a great god.

Cadmus

My boy,

Teiresias advises well. Your home is here   330
with us, with our customs and traditions, not
outside, alone. Your mind is distracted now,
and what you think is sheer delirium.
Even if this Dionysus is no god,
as you assert, persuade yourself that he is.
The fiction is a noble one, for Semele will seem   335
to be the mother of a god, and this confers
no small distinction on our family.

You saw

that dreadful death your cousin Actaeon died
when those man-eating hounds he had raised himself
savaged him and tore his body limb from limb
because he boasted that his prowess in the hunt surpassed   340
the skill of Artemis.

Do not let his fate be yours.

Here, let me wreathe your head with leaves of ivy.
Then come with us and glorify the god.

Pentheus

Take your hands off me! Go worship your Bacchus,
but do not wipe your madness off on me.
By god, I'll make him pay, the man who taught you   345
this folly of yours.

(*He turns to his attendants.*)

Go, someone, this instant,

to the place where this prophet prophesies.
Pry it up with crowbars, heave it over,
upside down; demolish everything you see.
Throw his fillets out to wind and weather.   350
That will provoke him more than anything.
As for the rest of you, go and scour the city
for that effeminate stranger, the man who infects our women
with this strange disease and pollutes our beds.

And when you take him, clap him in chains   355
and march him here. He shall die as he deserves—
by being stoned to death. He shall come to rue
his merrymaking here in Thebes.

(Exeunt attendants.)

Teiresias

                    Reckless fool,
you do not know the consequences of your words.
You talked madness before, but this is raving
lunacy!
              Cadmus, let us go and pray   360
for this raving fool and for this city too,
pray to the god that no awful vengeance strike
from heaven.
            Take your staff and follow me.
Support me with your hands, and I shall help you too
lest we stumble and fall, a sight of shame,
two old men together.
                 But go we must,   365
acknowledging the service that we owe to god,
Bacchus, the son of Zeus.
               And yet take care
lest someday your house repent of Pentheus
in its sufferings. I speak not prophecy
but fact. The words of fools finish in folly.

(Exeunt Teiresias and Cadmus. Pentheus
retires into the palace.)

Chorus

—Holiness, queen of heaven,   370
  Holiness on golden wing
  who hover over earth,
  do you hear what Pentheus says?
  Do you hear his blasphemy
  against the prince of the blessèd,   375
  the god of garlands and banquets,

Bromius, Semele's son?
These blessings he gave:
laughter to the flute   380
and the loosing of cares
when the shining wine is spilled
at the feast of the gods,
and the wine-bowl casts its sleep   385
on feasters crowned with ivy.

—A tongue without reins,
defiance, unwisdom—
their end is disaster.
But the life of quiet good,
the wisdom that accepts—   390
these abide unshaken,
preserving, sustaining
the houses of men.
Far in the air of heaven,
the sons of heaven live.
But they watch the lives of men.
And what passes for wisdom is not;   395
unwise are those who aspire,
who outrange the limits of man.
Briefly, we live. Briefly,
then die. Wherefore, I say,
he who hunts a glory, he who tracks
some boundless, superhuman dream,
may lose his harvest here and now
and garner death. Such men are mad,   400
    their counsels evil.

—O let me come to Cyprus,
island of Aphrodite,
homes of the loves that cast
their spells on the hearts of men!   405
Or Paphos where the hundred-
mouthed barbarian river

brings ripeness without rain!
To Pieria, haunt of the Muses, 410
and the holy hill of Olympus!
O Bromius, leader, god of joy,
Bromius, take me there!
There the lovely Graces go,
and there Desire, and there
the right is mine to worship 415
as I please.

—The deity, the son of Zeus,
in feast, in festival, delights.
He loves the goddess Peace,
generous of good,
preserver of the young. 420
To rich and poor he gives
the simple gift of wine,
the gladness of the grape.
But him who scoffs he hates,
and him who mocks his life,
the happiness of those
for whom the day is blessed 425
but doubly blessed the night;
whose simple wisdom shuns the thoughts
of proud, uncommon men and all
their god-encroaching dreams.
But what the common people do, 430
the things that simple men believe,
    I too believe and do.

(As Penthus reappears from the palace,
enter from the left several attendants
leading Dionysus captive.)

Attendant

Pentheus, here we are; not empty-handed either.
We captured the quarry you sent us out to catch. 435
But our prey here was tame: refused to run

or hide, held out his hands as willing as you please,
completely unafraid. His ruddy cheeks were flushed
as though with wine, and he stood there smiling,
making no objection when we roped his hands   440
and marched him here. It made me feel ashamed.
"Listen, stranger," I said, "I am not to blame.
We act under orders from Pentheus. He ordered
your arrest."

        As for those women you clapped in chains
and sent to the dungeon, they're gone, clean away,   445
went skipping off to the fields crying on their god
Bromius. The chains on their legs snapped apart
by themselves. Untouched by any human hand,
the doors swung wide, opening of their own accord.
Sir, this stranger who has come to Thebes is full   450
of many miracles. I know no more than that.
The rest is your affair.

Pentheus

        Untie his hands.
We have him in our net. He may be quick,
but he cannot escape us now, I think.

        (*While the servants untie Dionysus' hands, Pentheus
        attentively scrutinizes his prisoner. Then
        the servants step back, leaving Pentheus
        and Dionysus face to face.*)

        So,
you *are* attractive, stranger, at least to women—
which explains, I think, your presence here in Thebes.
Your curls are long. You do not wrestle, I take it.   455
And what fair skin you have—you must take care of it—
no daylight complexion; no, it comes from the night
when you hunt Aphrodite with your beauty.
        Now then,
who are you and from where?

Dionysus
It is nothing   460
to boast of and easily told. You have heard, I suppose,
of Mount Tmolus and her flowers?

Pentheus
I know the place.
It rings the city of Sardis.

Dionysus
I come from there.
My country is Lydia.

Pentheus
Who is this god whose worship
you have imported into Hellas?

Dionysus
Dionysus, the son of Zeus.   465
He initiated me.

Pentheus
You have some local Zeus
who spawns new gods?

Dionysus
He is the same as yours—
the Zeus who married Semele.

Pentheus
How did you see him?
In a dream or face to face?

Dionysus
Face to face.
He gave me his rites.

Pentheus
What form do they take,   470
these mysteries of yours?

Dionysus

It is forbidden
to tell the uninitiate.

Pentheus

Tell me the benefits
that those who know your mysteries enjoy.

Dionysus

I am forbidden to say. But they are worth knowing.

Pentheus

Your answers are designed to make me curious.

Dionysus

No: 475

our mysteries abhor an unbelieving man.

Pentheus

You say you saw the god. What form did he assume?

Dionysus

Whatever form he wished. The choice was his,
not mine.

Pentheus

You evade the question.

Dionysus

Talk sense to a fool
and he calls you foolish.

Pentheus

Have you introduced your rites   480
in other cities too? Or is Thebes the first?

Dionysus

Foreigners everywhere now dance for Dionysus.

Pentheus

They are more ignorant than Greeks.

Dionysus

In this matter
they are not. Customs differ.

Pentheus

Do you hold your rites
during the day or night?

Dionysus

Mostly by night.   485
The darkness is well suited to devotion.

Pentheus

Better suited to lechery and seducing women.

Dionysus

You can find debauchery by daylight too.

Pentheus

You shall regret these clever answers.

Dionysus

And you,
your stupid blasphemies.

Pentheus

What a bold bacchant!   490
You wrestle well—when it comes to words.

Dionysus

Tell me,
what punishment do you propose?

Pentheus

First of all,
I shall cut off your girlish curls.

Dionysus

My hair is holy.
My curls belong to god.

(*Pentheus shears away the god's curls.*)

Pentheus

Second, you will surrender
your wand.

Dionysus

You take it. It belongs to Dionysus.   495

(*Pentheus takes the thyrsus.*)

Pentheus

Last, I shall place you under guard and confine you
in the palace.

Dionysus

The god himself will set me free
whenever I wish.

Pentheus

You will be with your women in prison
when you call on him for help.

Dionysus

He is here now
and sees what I endure from you.

Pentheus

Where is he?   500
I cannot see him.

Dionysus

With me. Your blasphemies
have made you blind.

Pentheus (*to attendants*)

Seize him. He is mocking me
and Thebes.

Dionysus
> I give you sober warning, fools:
place no chains on *me*.

Pentheus
> But *I* say: chain him.
And I am the stronger here.

Dionysus
> You do not know   505
the limits of your strength. You do not know
what you do. You do not know who you are.

Pentheus

I am Pentheus, the son of Echion and Agave.

Dionysus

Pentheus: you shall repent that name.

Pentheus
> Off with him.
Chain his hands; lock him in the stables by the palace.
Since he desires the darkness, give him what he wants.   510
Let him dance down there in the dark.

> *(As the attendants bind Dionysus' hands, the Chorus
> beats on its drums with increasing agitation
> as though to emphasize the sacrilege.)*
> As for these women,
your accomplices in making trouble here,
I shall have them sold as slaves or put to work
at my looms. That will silence their drums.

> *(Exit Pentheus.)*

Dionysus
> I go,   515
though not to suffer, since that cannot be.
But Dionysus whom you outrage by your acts,

who you deny is god, will call you to account.
When you set chains on me, you manacle the god.

(*Exeunt attendants with Dionysus captive.*)

Chorus

—O Dirce, holy river,   520
    child of Achelöus' water,
    yours the springs that welcomed once
    divinity, the son of Zeus!
    For Zeus the father snatched his son
    from deathless flame, crying: 525
    Dithyrambus, come!
    Enter my male womb.
    I name you Bacchus and to Thebes
    proclaim you by that name.
    But now, O blessèd Dirce,   530
    you banish me when to your banks I come,
    crowned with ivy, bringing revels.
    O Dirce, why am I rejected?
    By the clustered grapes I swear,
    by Dionysus' wine,   535
    someday you shall come to know
        the name of *Bromius!*

—With fury, with fury, he rages,
    Pentheus, son of Echion,   540
    born of the breed of Earth,
    spawned by the dragon, whelped by Earth!
    Inhuman, a rabid beast,
    a giant in wildness raging,
    storming, defying the children of heaven.
    He has threatened me with bonds   545
    though my body is bound to god.
    He cages my comrades with chains;
    he has cast them in prison darkness.
    O lord, son of Zeus, do you see?   550

O Dionysus, do you see
how in shackles we are held
unbreakably, in the bonds of oppressors?
Descend from Olympus, lord!
Come, whirl your wand of gold
and quell with death this beast of blood   555
whose violence abuses man and god
   outrageously.

—O lord, where do you wave your wand
among the running companies of god?
There on Nysa, mother of beasts?
There on the ridges of Corycia?
Or there among the forests of Olympus   560
where Orpheus fingered his lyre
and mustered with music the trees,
mustered the wilderness beasts?
O Pieria, you are blessed!   565
Evius honors you. He comes to dance,
bringing his Bacchae, fording the race
where Axios runs, bringing his Maenads   570
whirling over Lydias,
generous father of rivers
and famed for his lovely waters
that fatten a land of good horses.   575

        (Thunder and lightning. The earth trembles.
            The Chorus is crazed with fear.)

Dionysus (from within)
  Ho!
  Hear me! Ho, Bacchae!
  Ho, Bacchae! Hear my cry!

Chorus
  Who cries?
  Who calls me with that cry
  of Evius? Where are you, lord?

Dionysus

> Ho! Again I cry—   580
> the son of Zeus and Semele!

Chorus

> O lord, lord Bromius!
> Bromius, come to us now!

Dionysus

> *Let the earthquake come! Shatter the floor of the world!*   585

Chorus

> —Look there, how the palace of Pentheus totters.
> —Look, the palace is collapsing!
> —Dionysus is within. Adore him!
> —We adore him!   590
> —Look there!
>   —Above the pillars, how the great stones
>   gape and crack!
>   —Listen. Bromius cries his victory!

Dionysus

> *Launch the blazing thunderbolt of god! O lightnings,*
> *come! Consume with flame the palace of Pentheus!*   595

>   (*A burst of lightning flares across the façade of the palace*
>   *and tongues of flame spurt up from the tomb of*
>   *Semele. Then a great crash of thunder.*)

Chorus

> Ah,
> look how the fire leaps up
> on the holy tomb of Semele,
> the flame of Zeus of Thunders,
> his lightnings, still alive,
> blazing where they fell!
> Down, Maenads,   600
> fall to the ground in awe! He walks
> among the ruins he has made!

He has brought the high house low!
He comes, our god, the son of Zeus!

*(The Chorus falls to the ground in oriental fashion, bowing
their heads in the direction of the palace. A hush;
then Dionysus appears, lightly picking his way
among the rubble. Calm and smiling still,
he speaks to the Chorus with a solic-
itude approaching banter.)*

Dionysus

What, women of Asia? Were you so overcome with fright
you fell to the ground? I think then you must have seen   605
how Bacchus jostled the palace of Pentheus. But come, rise.
Do not be afraid.

Coryphaeus

O greatest light of our holy revels,
how glad I am to see your face! Without you I was lost.

Dionysus

Did you despair when they led me away to cast me down   610
in the darkness of Pentheus' prison?

Coryphaeus

What else could I do?
Where would I turn for help if something happened to you?
But how did you escape that godless man?

Dionysus

With ease.
No effort was required.

Coryphaeus

But the manacles on your wrists?   615

Dionysus

There I, in turn, humiliated him, outrage for outrage.
He seemed to think that he was chaining me but never once

so much as touched my hands. He fed on his desires.
Inside the stable he intended as my jail, instead of me,
he found a bull and tried to rope its knees and hooves.
He was panting desperately, biting his lips with his teeth, 620
his whole body drenched with sweat, while I sat nearby,
quietly watching. But at that moment Bacchus came,
shook the palace and touched his mother's grave with tongues
of fire. Imagining the palace was in flames,
Pentheus went rushing here and there, shouting to his slaves 625
to bring him water. Every hand was put to work: in vain.
Then, afraid I might escape, he suddenly stopped short,
drew his sword and rushed to the palace. There, it seems,
Bromius had made a shape, a phantom which resembled me, 630
within the court. Bursting in, Pentheus thrust and stabbed
at that thing of gleaming air as though he thought it me.
And then, once again, the god humiliated him.
He razed the palace to the ground where it lies, shattered
in utter ruin—his reward for my imprisonment.
At that bitter sight, Pentheus dropped his sword, exhausted 635
by the struggle. A man, a man, and nothing more,
yet he presumed to wage a war with god.

                         For my part,
I left the palace quietly and made my way outside.
For Pentheus I care nothing.

                        But judging from the sound
of tramping feet inside the court, I think our man
will soon be here. What, I wonder, will he have to say? 640
But let him bluster. I shall not be touched to rage.
Wise men know constraint: our passions are controlled.

        (*Enter Pentheus, stamping heavily, from the ruined palace.*)
Pentheus

But this is mortifying. That stranger, that man
I clapped in irons, has escaped.

                    (*He catches sight of Dionysus.*)

What! *You?* 645
Well, what do you have to say for yourself?
How did you escape? Answer me.

Dionysus

Your anger
walks too heavily. Tread lightly here.

Pentheus

How did you escape?

Dionysus

Don't you remember?
Someone, I said, would set me free.

Pentheus

Someone? 650
But who? Who is this mysterious someone?

Dionysus

[He who makes the grape grow its clusters
for mankind.]

Pentheus

A splendid contribution, that.

Dionysus

You disparage the gift that is his chiefest glory.

Pentheus

[If I catch him here, he will not escape my anger.]
I shall order every gate in every tower
to be bolted tight.

Dionysus

And so? Could not a god
hurdle your city walls?

Pentheus

You are clever—very— 655
but not where it counts.

Dionysus
Where it counts the most,

there I *am* clever.

(Enter a messenger, a herdsman from Mount Cithaeron.)

But hear this messenger

who brings you news from the mountain of Cithaeron.
We shall remain where we are. Do not fear:
we will not run away.

Messenger
Pentheus, king of Thebes,

660

I come from Cithaeron where the gleaming flakes of snow
fall on and on forever—

Pentheus
Get to the point.

What is your message, man?

Messenger
Sir, I have seen

the holy Maenads, the women who ran barefoot   665
and crazy from the city, and I wanted to report
to you and Thebes what weird fantastic things,
what miracles and more than miracles,
these women do. But may I speak freely
in my own way and words, or make it short?
I fear the harsh impatience of your nature, sire,   670
too kingly and too quick to anger.

Pentheus
Speak freely.

You have my promise: I shall not punish you.
Displeasure with a man who speaks the truth is wrong.
However, the more terrible this tale of yours,
that much more terrible will be the punishment   675
I impose upon that man who taught our womenfolk
this strange new magic.

Messenger
                         About that hour
when the sun lets loose its light to warm the earth,
our grazing herds of cows had just begun to climb
the path along the mountain ridge. Suddenly
I saw three companies of dancing women,   680
one led by Autonoë, the second captained
by your mother Agave, while Ino led the third.
There they lay in the deep sleep of exhaustion,
some resting on boughs of fir, others sleeping
where they fell, here and there among the oak leaves—   685
but all modestly and soberly, not, as you think,
drunk with wine, nor wandering, led astray
by the music of the flute, to hunt their Aphrodite
through the woods.
                         But your mother heard the lowing
of our hornèd herds, and springing to her feet,   690
gave a great cry to waken them from sleep.
And they too, rubbing the bloom of soft sleep
from their eyes, rose up lightly and straight—
a lovely sight to see: all as one,
the old women and the young and the unmarried girls.
First they let their hair fall loose, down   695
over their shoulders, and those whose straps had slipped
fastened their skins of fawn with writhing snakes
that licked their cheeks. Breasts swollen with milk,
new mothers who had left their babies behind at home
nestled gazelles and young wolves in their arms,   700
suckling them. Then they crowned their hair with leaves,
ivy and oak and flowering bryony. One woman
struck her thyrsus against a rock and a fountain
of cool water came bubbling up. Another drove   705
her fennel in the ground, and where it struck the earth,
at the touch of god, a spring of wine poured out.
Those who wanted milk scratched at the soil
with bare fingers and the white milk came welling up.   710

Pure honey spurted, streaming, from their wands.
If you had been there and seen these wonders for yourself,
you would have gone down on your knees and prayed
to the god you now deny.

                    We cowherds and shepherds
gathered in small groups, wondering and arguing   715
among ourselves at these fantastic things,
the awful miracles those women did.
But then a city fellow with the knack of words
rose to his feet and said: "All you who live
upon the pastures of the mountain, what do you say?
Shall we earn a little favor with King Pentheus   720
by hunting his mother Agave out of the revels?"
Falling in with his suggestion, we withdrew
and set ourselves in ambush, hidden by the leaves
among the undergrowth. Then at a signal
all the Bacchae whirled their wands for the revels
to begin. With one voice they cried aloud:
"*O Iacchus! Son of Zeus!*" "*O Bromius!*" they cried   725
until the beasts and all the mountain seemed
wild with divinity. And when they ran,
everything ran with them.

                    It happened, however,
that Agave ran near the ambush where I lay
concealed. Leaping up, I tried to seize her,   730
but she gave a cry: "Hounds who run with me,
men are hunting us down! Follow, follow me!
Use your wands for weapons."

                    At this we fled
and barely missed being torn to pieces by the women.
Unarmed, they swooped down upon the herds of cattle   735
grazing there on the green of the meadow. And then
you could have seen a single woman with bare hands
tear a fat calf, still bellowing with fright,
in two, while others clawed the heifers to pieces.
There were ribs and cloven hooves scattered everywhere,   740

and scraps smeared with blood hung from the fir trees.
And bulls, their raging fury gathered in their horns,
lowered their heads to charge, then fell, stumbling
to the earth, pulled down by hordes of women   745
and stripped of flesh and skin more quickly, sire,
than you could blink your royal eyes. Then,
carried up by their own speed, they flew like birds
across the spreading fields along Asopus' stream
where most of all the ground is good for harvesting.   750
Like invaders they swooped on Hysiae
and on Erythrae in the foothills of Cithaeron.
Everything in sight they pillaged and destroyed.
They snatched the children from their homes. And when
they piled their plunder on their backs, it stayed in place,   755
untied. Nothing, neither bronze nor iron,
fell to the dark earth. Flames flickered
in their curls and did not burn them. Then the villagers,
furious at what the women did, took to arms.
And *there*, sire, was something terrible to see.   760
For the men's spears were pointed and sharp, and yet
drew no blood, whereas the wands the women threw
inflicted wounds. And then the men *ran*,
routed by women! Some god, I say, was with them.
The Bacchae then returned where they had started,   765
by the springs the god had made, and washed their hands
while the snakes licked away the drops of blood
that dabbled their cheeks.
                        Whoever this god may be,
sire, welcome him to Thebes. For he is great
in many other ways as well. It was he,   770
or so they say, who gave to mortal men
the gift of lovely wine by which our suffering
is stopped. And if there is no god of wine,
there is no love, no Aphrodite either,
nor other pleasure left to men.
                                        (*Exit messenger.*)

Coryphaeus

                                I tremble   775
to speak the words of freedom before the tyrant.
But let the truth be told: there is no god
greater than Dionysus.

Pentheus

                       Like a blazing fire
this Bacchic violence spreads. It comes too close.
We are disgraced, humiliated in the eyes
of Hellas. This is no time for hesitation.   780

                            (*He turns to an attendant.*)

You there. Go down quickly to the Electran gates
and order out all heavy-armored infantry;
call up the fastest troops among our cavalry,
the mobile squadrons and the archers. We march
against the Bacchae! Affairs are out of hand   785
when we tamely endure such conduct in our women.

                                (*Exit attendant.*)

Dionysus

Pentheus, you do not hear, or else you disregard
my words of warning. You have done me wrong,
and yet, in spite of that, I warn you once
again: do not take arms against a god.
Stay quiet here. Bromius will not let you   790
drive his women from their revels on the mountain.

Pentheus

Don't you lecture me. You escaped from prison.
Or shall I punish you again?

Dionysus

                         If I were you,
I would offer him a sacrifice, not rage
and kick against necessity, a man defying   795
god.

Pentheus

     I shall give your god the sacrifice
that he deserves. His victims will be his women.
I shall make a great slaughter in the woods of Cithaeron.

Dionysus

    You will all be routed, shamefully defeated,
when their wands of ivy turn back your shields
of bronze.

Pentheus

        It is hopeless to wrestle with this man.   800
Nothing on earth will make him hold his tongue.

Dionysus

                             Friend,
you can still save the situation.

Pentheus

              How?
By accepting orders from my own slaves?

Dionysus

                No.
I undertake to lead the women back to Thebes.
Without bloodshed.

Pentheus

         This is some trap.

Dionysus

                 A trap?   805
How so, if I save you by my own devices?

Pentheus

               I know.
You and they have conspired to establish your rites
forever.

Dionysus

    True, I *have* conspired—with god.

Pentheus

Bring my armor, someone. And *you* stop talking.   810

> (*Pentheus strides toward the left, but when he is almost*
> *offstage, Dionysus calls imperiously to him.*)

Dionysus

Wait!
Would you like to *see* their revels on the mountain?

Pentheus

I would pay a great sum to see that sight.

Dionysus

Why are you so passionately curious?

Pentheus

Of course
I'd be sorry to see them drunk—

Dionysus

But for all your sorrow,   815
you'd like very much to see them?

Pentheus

Yes, very much.
I could crouch beneath the fir trees, out of sight.

Dionysus

But if you try to hide, they may track you down.

Pentheus

Your point is well taken. I will go openly.

Dionysus

Shall I lead you there now? Are you ready to go?

Pentheus

The sooner the better. The loss of even a moment   820
would be disappointing now.

Dionysus
                    First, however,
you must dress yourself in women's clothes.

Pentheus
                                        What?
You want *me*, a man, to wear a woman's dress. But why?

Dionysus
If they knew you were a man, they would kill you instantly.

Pentheus
True. You are an old hand at cunning, I see.

Dionysus
Dionysus taught me everything I know.   825

Pentheus
Your advice is to the point. What I fail to see
is what we do.

Dionysus
                    I shall go inside with you
and help you dress.

Pentheus
                    Dress? In a *woman's* dress,
you mean? I would die of shame.

Dionysus
                              Very well.
Then you no longer hanker to see the Maenads?

Pentheus
What is this costume I must wear?

Dionysus
                                   On your head   830
I shall set a wig with long curls.

Pentheus

And then?

Dionysus

Next, robes to your feet and a net for your hair.

Pentheus

Yes? Go on.

Dionysus

Then a thyrsus for your hand
and a skin of dappled fawn.

Pentheus

I could not bear it.   835
I *cannot* bring myself to dress in women's clothes.

Dionysus

Then you must fight the Bacchae. That means bloodshed.

Pentheus

Right. First we must go and reconnoiter.

Dionysus

Surely a wiser course than that of hunting bad
with worse.

Pentheus

But how can we pass through the city
without being seen?

Dionysus

We shall take deserted streets.   840
I will lead the way.

Pentheus

Any way you like,
provided those women of Bacchus don't jeer at me.
First, however, I shall ponder your advice,
whether to go or not.

Dionysus

Do as you please.
I am ready, whatever you decide.

Pentheus

Yes.
Either I shall march with my army to the mountain   845
or act on your advice.

(Exit Pentheus into the palace.)

Dionysus

Women, our prey now thrashes
in the net we threw. He shall see the Bacchae
and pay the price with death.

O Dionysus,
now action rests with you. And you are near.
Punish this man. But first distract his wits;   850
bewilder him with madness. For sane of mind
this man would never wear a woman's dress;
but obsess his soul and he will not refuse.
After those threats with which he was so fierce,
I want him made the laughingstock of Thebes,
paraded through the streets, a woman.

Now   855
I shall go and costume Pentheus in the clothes
which he must wear to Hades when he dies, butchered
by the hands of his mother. He shall come to know
Dionysus, son of Zeus, consummate god,   860
most terrible, and yet most gentle, to mankind.

(Exit Dionysus into the palace.)

Chorus

—When shall I dance once more
with bare feet the all-night dances,
tossing my head for joy
in the damp air, in the dew,   865
as a running fawn might frisk
for the green joy of the wide fields,

free from fear of the hunt,
free from the circling beaters
and the nets of woven mesh
and the hunters hallooing on
their yelping packs? And then, hard pressed,
she sprints with the quickness of wind,
bounding over the marsh, leaping
to frisk, leaping for joy,
gay with the green of the leaves,
to dance for joy in the forest,
to dance where the darkness is deepest,
    where no man is.

—What is wisdom? What gift of the gods
is held in honor like this:
to hold your hand victorious
over the heads of those you hate?
Honor is precious forever.

—Slow but unmistakable
the might of the gods moves on.
It punishes that man,
infatuate of soul
and hardened in his pride,
who disregards the gods.
The gods are crafty:
they lie in ambush
a long step of time
to hunt the unholy.
Beyond the old beliefs,
no thought, no act shall go.
Small, small is the cost
to believe in this:
whatever is god is strong;
whatever long time has sanctioned,
that is a law forever;
the law tradition makes
is the law of nature.

870

875

880

885

890

895

—What is wisdom? What gift of the gods
is held in honor like this:
to hold your hand victorious
over the heads of those you hate?   900
Honor is precious forever.

—Blessèd is he who escapes a storm at sea,
        who comes home to his harbor.
—Blessèd is he who emerges from under affliction.
—In various ways one man outraces another in the
        race for wealth and power.   905
—Ten thousand men possess ten thousand hopes.
—A few bear fruit in happiness; the others go awry.
—But he who garners day by day the good of life,   910
        he is happiest. Blessèd is he.

*(Re-enter Dionysus from the palace. At the threshold
he turns and calls back to Pentheus.)*

Dionysus

Pentheus if you are still so curious to see
forbidden sights, so bent on evil still,
come out. Let us see you in your woman's dress,
disguised in Maenad clothes so you may go and spy   915
upon your mother and her company.

*(Enter Pentheus from the palace. He wears a long linen dress
which partially conceals his fawn-skin. He carries a thyrsus
in his hand; on his head he wears a wig with long blond
curls bound by a snood. He is dazed and completely in
the power of the god who has now possessed him.)*

                                Why,
you look exactly like one of the daughters of Cadmus.

Pentheus

I seem to see two suns blazing in the heavens.
And now two Thebes, two cities, and each
with seven gates. And you—you are a bull   920

who walks before me there. Horns have sprouted
from your head. Have you always been a beast?
But now I see a bull.

Dionysus

It is the god you see.
Though hostile formerly, he now declares a truce
and goes with us. You see what you could not
when you were blind.

Pentheus (coyly primping)

Do I look like anyone?   925
Like Ino or my mother Agave?

Dionysus

So much alike
I almost might be seeing one of them. But look:
one of your curls has come loose from under the snood
where I tucked it.

Pentheus

It must have worked loose
when I was dancing for joy and shaking my head.   930

Dionysus

Then let me be your maid and tuck it back.
Hold still.

Pentheus

Arrange it. I am in your hands
completely.

(Dionysus tucks the curl back under the snood.)

Dionysus

And now your strap has slipped. Yes,   935
and your robe hangs askew at the ankles.

Pentheus (bending backward to look)

I think so.
At least on my right leg. But on the left the hem
lies straight.

Dionysus
You will think me the best of friends
when you see to your surprise how chaste the Bacchae are.   940

Pentheus
But to be a real Bacchante, should I hold
the wand in my right hand? Or this way?

Dionysus
No.
In your right hand. And raise it as you raise
your right foot. I commend your change of heart.

Pentheus
Could I lift Cithaeron up, do you think?   945
Shoulder the cliffs, Bacchae and all?

Dionysus
If you wanted.
Your mind was once unsound, but now you think
as sane men do.

Pentheus
Should we take crowbars with us?
Or should I put my shoulder to the cliffs   950
and heave them up?

Dionysus
What? And destroy the haunts
of the nymphs, the holy groves where Pan plays
his woodland pipe?

Pentheus
You are right. In any case,
women should not be mastered by brute strength.
I will hide myself beneath the firs instead.

Dionysus
You will find all the ambush you deserve,   955
creeping up to spy on the Maenads.

Pentheus

Think.
I can see them already, there among the bushes,
mating like birds, caught in the toils of love.

Dionysus

Exactly. This is your mission: you go to watch.
You may surprise them—or they may surprise you.   960

Pentheus

Then lead me through the very heart of Thebes,
since I, alone of all this city, dare to go.

Dionysus

You and you alone will suffer for your city.
A great ordeal awaits you. But you are worthy
of your fate. I shall lead you safely there;   965
someone else shall bring you back.

Pentheus

Yes, my mother.

Dionysus

An example to all men.

Pentheus

It is for that I go.

Dionysus

You will be carried home—

Pentheus

O luxury!

Dionysus

cradled in your mother's arms.

Pentheus

You will spoil me.

Dionysus

I *mean* to spoil you.

Pentheus

I go to my reward. 970

Dionysus

You are an extraordinary young man, and you go
to an extraordinary experience. You shall win
a glory towering to heaven and usurping
god's.

(*Exit Pentheus.*)

Agave and you daughters of Cadmus,
reach out your hands! I bring this young man
to a great ordeal. The victor? Bromius. 975
Bromius—and I. The rest the event shall show.

(*Exit Dionysus.*)

Chorus

—Run to the mountain, fleet hounds of madness!
Run, run to the revels of Cadmus' daughters!
Sting them against the man in women's clothes, 980
the madman who spies on the Maenads, who peers
from behind the rocks, who spies from a vantage!
His mother shall see him first. She will cry 985
to the Maenads: "Who is this spy who has come
to the mountains to peer at the mountain-revels
of the women of Thebes? What bore him, Bacchae?
This man was born of no woman. Some lioness
give him birth, some one of the Libyan gorgons!" 990

—O Justice, principle of order, spirit of custom,
come! Be manifest; reveal yourself with a sword!
Stab through the throat that godless man,
the mocker who goes, flouting custom and outraging god!
O Justice, stab the evil earth-born spawn of Echion! 995

—Uncontrollable, the unbeliever goes,
in spitting rage, rebellious and amok,
madly assaulting the mysteries of god,
profaning the rites of the mother of god.

Against the unassailable he runs, with rage   1000
obsessed. Headlong he runs to death.
For death the gods exact, curbing by that bit
the mouths of men. They humble us with death
that we remember what we are who are not god,
but men. We run to death. Wherefore, I say,
accept, accept:
humility is wise; humility is blest.
But what the world calls wise I do not want.   1005
Elsewhere the chase. I hunt another game,
those great, those manifest, those certain goals,
achieving which, our mortal lives are blest.
Let these things be the quarry of my chase:
purity; humility; an unrebellious soul,
accepting all. Let me go the customary way,
the timeless, honored, beaten path of those who walk
with reverence and awe beneath the sons of heaven.   1010

—O Justice, principle of order, spirit of custom,
come! Be manifest; reveal yourself with a sword!
Stab through the throat that godless man,
the mocker who goes, flouting custom and outraging god!
O Justice, destroy the evil earth-born sprawn of Echion!   1015

—O Dionysus, reveal yourself a bull! Be manifest,
a snake with darting heads, a lion breathing fire!
O Bacchus, come! Come with your smile!
Cast your noose about this man who hunts
your Bacchae! Bring him down, trampled   1020
underfoot by the murderous herd of your Maenads!

(Enter a messenger from Cithaeron.)

Messenger

How prosperous in Hellas these halls once were,
this house founded by Cadmus, the stranger from Sidon   1025
who sowed the dragon seed in the land of the snake!

I am a slave and nothing more, yet even so
I mourn the fortunes of this fallen house.

Coryphaeus

         What is it?
Is there news of the Bacchae?

Messenger

      This is my news:
Pentheus, the son of Echion, is dead.   1030

Coryphaeus

All hail to Bromius! Our god is a great god!

Messenger

What is this you say, women? You dare to rejoice
at these disasters which destroy this house?

Coryphaeus

I am no Greek. I hail my god
in my own way. No longer need I
shrink with fear of prison.   1035

Messenger

If you suppose this city is so short of men—

Coryphaeus

Dionysus, Dionysus, not Thebes,
has power over me.

Messenger

Your feelings might be forgiven, then. But this,
this exultation in disaster—it is not right.   1040

Coryphaeus

Tell us how the mocker died.
How was he killed?

Messenger

    There were three of us in all: Pentheus and I,
attending my master, and that stranger who volunteered
his services as guide. Leaving behind us
the last outlying farms of Thebes, we forded
the Asopus and struck into the barren scrubland   1045
of Cithaeron.

            There in a grassy glen we halted,
unmoving, silent, without a word,
so we might see but not be seen. From that vantage,   1050
in a hollow cut from the sheer rock of the cliffs,
a place where water ran and the pines grew dense
with shade, we saw the Maenads sitting, their hands
busily moving at their happy tasks. Some
wound the stalks of their tattered wands with tendrils   1055
of fresh ivy; others, frisking like fillies
newly freed from the painted bridles, chanted
in Bacchic songs, responsively.

                But Pentheus—
unhappy man—could not quite see the companies
of women. "Stranger," he said, "from where I stand,
I cannot see these counterfeited Maenads.   1060
But if I climbed that towering fir that overhangs
the banks, then I could see their shameless orgies
better."

         And now the stranger worked a miracle.
Reaching for the highest branch of a great fir,
he bent it down, down, down to the dark earth,   1065
till it was curved the way a taut bow bends
or like a rim of wood when forced about the circle
of a wheel. Like that he forced that mountain fir
down to the ground. No mortal could have done it.
Then he seated Pentheus at the highest tip   1070
and with his hands let the trunk rise straightly up,
slowly and gently, lest it throw its rider.
And the tree rose, towering to heaven, with my master

huddled at the top. And now the Maenads saw him
more clearly than he saw them. But barely had they seen,   1075
when the stranger vanished and there came a great voice
out of heaven—Dionysus', it must have been—
crying: "Women, I bring you the man who has mocked
at you and me and at our holy mysteries.   1080
Take vengeance upon him." And as he spoke
a flash of awful fire bound earth and heaven.
The high air hushed, and along the forest glen
the leaves hung still; you could hear no cry of beasts.   1085
The Bacchae heard that voice but missed its words,
and leaping up, they stared, peering everywhere.
Again that voice. And now they knew his cry,
the clear command of god. And breaking loose
like startled doves, through grove and torrent,   1090
over jagged rocks, they flew, their feet maddened
by the breath of god. And when they saw my master
perching in his tree, they climbed a great stone   1095
that towered opposite his perch and showered him
with stones and javelins of fir, while the others
hurled their wands. And yet they missed their target,
poor Pentheus in his perch, barely out of reach   1100
of their eager hands, treed, unable to escape.
Finally they splintered branches from the oaks
and with those bars of wood tried to lever up the tree
by prying at the roots. But every effort failed.   1105
Then Agave cried out: "Maenads, make a circle
about the trunk and grip it with your hands.
Unless we take this climbing beast, he will reveal
the secrets of the god." With that, thousands of hands
tore the fir tree from the earth, and down, down   1110
from his high perch fell Pentheus, tumbling
to the ground, sobbing and screaming as he fell,
for he knew his end was near. His own mother,
like a priestess with her victim, fell upon him
first. But snatching off his wig and snood   1115

so she would recognize his face, he touched her cheeks,
screaming, *"No, no, Mother! I am Pentheus,*
your own son, the child you bore to Echion!
Pity me, spare me, Mother! I have done a wrong,   1120
but do not kill your own son for my offense."
But she was foaming at the mouth, and her crazed eyes
rolling with frenzy. She was mad, stark mad,
possessed by Bacchus. Ignoring his cries of pity,
she seized his left arm at the wrist; then, planting   1125
her foot upon his chest, she pulled, wrenching away
the arm at the shoulder—not by her own strength,
for the god had put inhuman power in her hands.
Ino, meanwhile, on the other side, was scratching off
his flesh. Then Autonoë and the whole horde   1130
of Bacchae swarmed upon him. Shouts everywhere,
he screaming with what little breath was left,
they shrieking in triumph. One tore off an arm,
another a foot still warm in its shoe. His ribs
were clawed clean of flesh and every hand   1135
was smeared with blood as they played ball with scraps
of Pentheus' body.

        The pitiful remains lie scattered,
one piece among the sharp rocks, others
lying lost among the leaves in the depths
of the forest. His mother, picking up his head,   1140
impaled it on her wand. She seems to think it is
some mountain lion's head which she carries in triumph
through the thick of Cithaeron. Leaving her sisters
at the Maenad dances, she is coming here, gloating
over her grisly prize. She calls upon Bacchus: 1145
he is her "fellow-huntsman," "comrade of the chase,
crowned with victory." But all the victory
she carries home is her own grief.

                Now,
before Agave returns, let me leave
this scene of sorrow. Humility,

a sense of reverence before the sons of heaven—   1150
of all the prizes that a mortal man might win,
these, I say, are wisest; these are best.

(Exit Messenger.)

Chorus

  —We dance to the glory of Bacchus!
    We dance to the death of Pentheus,
    the death of the spawn of the dragon!   1155
      He dressed in woman's dress;
      he took the lovely thyrsus;
      it waved him down to death,
        led by a bull to Hades.
    Hail, Bacchae! Hail, women of Thebes!   1160
    Your victory is fair, fair the prize,
      this famous prize of grief!
    Glorious the game! To fold your child
    in your arms, streaming with his blood!

Coryphaeus

  But look: there comes Pentheus' mother, Agave,   1165
  running wild-eyed toward the palace.
               —Welcome,
  welcome to the reveling band of the god of joy!

    (Enter Agave with other Bacchantes. She is covered with blood
    and carries the head of Pentheus impaled upon her thyrsus.)

Agave

  Bacchae of Asia—

Chorus

           Speak, speak.

Agave

  We bring this branch to the palace,
  this fresh-cut spray from the mountains.   1170
  Happy was the hunting.

« 243 »

Chorus

I see.
I welcome our fellow-reveler of god.

Agave

The whelp of a wild mountain lion,
and snared by me without a noose.
Look, look at the prize I bring.   1175

Chorus

Where was he caught?

Agave

On Cithaeron—

Chorus

On Cithaeron?

Agave

Our prize was killed.

Chorus

Who killed him?

Agave

I struck him first.
The Maenads call me "Agave the blest."   1180

Chorus

And then?

Agave

Cadmus'—

Chorus

Cadmus'?

Agave

Daughters.

After me, they reached the prey.
After me. Happy was the hunting.

Chorus

Happy indeed.

Agave

    Then share my glory,
share the feast.

Chorus

    Share, unhappy woman?

Agave

See, the whelp is young and tender.   1185
Beneath the soft mane of its hair,
the down is blooming on the cheeks.

Chorus

With that mane he *looks* a beast.

Agave

Our god is wise. Cunningly, cleverly,   1190
Bacchus the hunter lashed the Maenads
against his prey.

Chorus

    Our king is a hunter.

Agave

You praise me now?

Chorus

    I praise you.

Agave

The men of Thebes—

Chorus

    And Pentheus, your son?

Agave

Will praise his mother. She caught   1195
a great quarry, this lion's cub.

Chorus

Extraordinary catch.

Agave

Extraordinary skill.

Chorus

You are proud?

Agave

Proud and happy.
I have won the trophy of the chase,
a great prize, manifest to all.

Coryphaeus

Then, poor woman, show the citizens of Thebes   1200
this great prize, this trophy you have won
in the hunt.

(*Agave proudly exhibits her thyrsus with the head
of Pentheus impaled upon the point.*)

Agave

You citizens of this towered city,
men of Thebes, behold the trophy of your women's
hunting! *This* is the quarry of our chase, taken
not with nets nor spears of bronze but by the white   1205
and delicate hands of women. What are they worth,
your boastings now and all that uselessness
your armor is, since we, with our bare hands,
captured this quarry and tore its bleeding body
limb from limb?
—But where is my father Cadmus?   1210
He should come. And my son. Where is Pentheus?
Fetch him. I will have him set his ladder up
against the wall and, there upon the beam,
nail the head of this wild lion I have killed
as a trophy of my hunt.

(*Enter Cadmus, followed by attendants who bear upon
a bier the dismembered body of Pentheus.*)

Cadmus

      Follow me, attendants.   1215
Bear your dreadful burden in and set it down,
there before the palace.

      (The attendants set down the bier.)

     This was Pentheus
whose body, after long and weary searchings
I painfully assembled from Cithaeron's glens
where it lay, scattered in shreds, dismembered
throughout the forest, no two pieces   1220
in a single place.
     Old Teiresias and I
had returned to Thebes from the orgies on the mountain
before I learned of this atrocious crime
my daughters did. And so I hurried back
to the mountain to recover the body of this boy   1225
murdered by the Maenads. There among the oaks
I found Aristaeus' wife, the mother of Actaeon,
Autonoë, and with her Ino, both
still stung with madness. But Agave, they said,
was on her way to Thebes, still possessed.   1230
And what they said was true, for there she is,
and not a happy sight.

Agave

      Now, Father,
yours can be the proudest boast of living men.
For you are now the father of the bravest daughters
in the world. All of your daughters are brave,   1235
but I above the rest. I have left my shuttle
at the loom; I raised my sight to higher things—
to hunting animals with my bare hands.
       You see?
Here in my hands I hold the quarry of my chase,
a trophy for our house. Take it, Father, take it.   1240
Glory in my kill and invite your friends to share

the feast of triumph. For you are blest, Father,
by this great deed I have done.

Cadmus

This is a grief
so great it knows no size. I cannot look.
This is the awful murder your hands have done.   1245
This, *this* is the noble victim you have slaughtered
to the gods. And to share a feast like this
you now invite all Thebes and me?

O gods,
how terribly I pity you and then myself.
Justly—too, too justly—has lord Bromius,
this god of our own blood, destroyed us all,   1250
every one.

Agave

How scowling and crabbed is old age
in men. I hope my son takes after his mother
and wins, as she has done, the laurels of the chase
when he goes hunting with the younger men of Thebes.
But all my son can do is quarrel with god.   1255
He should be scolded, Father, and you are the one
who should scold him. Yes, someone call him out
so he can see his mother's triumph.

Cadmus

Enough. No more.
When you realize the horror you have done,
you shall suffer terribly. But if with luck   1260
your present madness lasts until you die,
you will seem to have, not having, happiness.

Agave

Why do you reproach me? Is there something wrong?

Cadmus

First raise your eyes to the heavens.

Agave
                              There.   1265
    But why?

Cadmus
              Does it look the same as it did before?
    Or has it changed?

Agave
                    It seems—somehow—clearer,
    brighter than it was before.

Cadmus
                        Do you still feel
    the same flurry inside you?

Agave
                        The same—flurry?
    No, I feel—somehow—calmer. I feel as though—   1270
    my mind were somehow—changing.

Cadmus
                            Can you still hear me?
    Can you answer clearly?

Agave
                        No. I have forgotten
    what we were saying, Father.

Cadmus
                            Who was your husband?

Agave
    Echion—a man, they said, born of the dragon seed.

Cadmus
    What was the name of the child you bore your husband?   1275

Agave
    Pentheus.

Cadmus
> And whose head do you hold in your hands?

Agave (averting her eyes)
> A lion's head—or so the hunters told me.

Cadmus
> Look directly at it. Just a quick glance.

Agave
> What is it? What am I holding in my hands?   1280

Cadmus
> Look more closely still. Study it carefully.

Agave
> *No!* O gods, I see the greatest grief there is.

Cadmus
> Does it look like a lion now?

Agave
> No, no. It is—
> Pentheus' head—I hold—

Cadmus
> And mourned by me   1285
> before you ever knew.

Agave
> But *who* killed him?
> Why am *I* holding him?

Cadmus
> O savage truth,
> what a time to come!

Agave
> For god's sake, speak.
> My heart is beating with terror.

Cadmus

You killed him.
You and your sisters.

Agave

But where was he killed?   1290
Here at home? Where?

Cadmus

He was killed on Cithaeron,
there where the hounds tore Actaeon to pieces.

Agave

But why? Why had Pentheus gone to Cithaeron?

Cadmus

He went to your revels to mock the god.

Agave

But *we*—
what were we doing on the mountain?

Cadmus

You were mad.   1295
The whole city was possessed.

Agave

Now, now I see:
Dionysus has destroyed us all.

Cadmus

You outraged him.
You denied that he was truly god.

Agave

Father,
where is my poor boy's body now?

Cadmus

There it is.
I gathered the pieces with great difficulty.

Agave

    Is his body entire? Has he been laid out well?   1300

Cadmus

    [All but the head. The rest is mutilated
    horribly.]

Agave

          But why should Pentheus suffer for my crime?

Cadmus

    He, like you, blasphemed the god. And so
    the god has brought us all to ruin at one blow,
    you, your sisters, and this boy. All our house
    the god as utterly destroyed and, with it,
    me. For I have no sons left, no male heir;   1305
    and I have lived only to see this boy,
    this branch of your own body, most horribly
    and foully killed.

                  (He turns and addresses the corpse.)

          —To you my house looked up.
    Child, you were the stay of my house; you were
    my daughter's son. Of you this city stood in awe.   1310
    No one who once had seen your face dared outrage
    the old man, or if he did, you punished him.
    Now I must go, a banished and dishonored man—
    I, Cadmus the great, who sowed the soldiery
    of Thebes and harvested a great harvest. My son,   1315
    dearest to me of all men—for even dead,
    I count you still the man I love the most—
    never again will your hand touch my chin;
    no more, child, will you hug me and call me
    "Grandfather" and say, "Who is wronging you?   1320
    Does anyone trouble you or vex your heart, old man?
    Tell me, Grandfather, and I will punish him."
    No, now there is grief for me; the mourning

for you; pity for your mother; and for her sisters,
sorrow.
          If there is still any mortal man   1325
who despises or defies the gods, let him look
on this boy's death and believe in the gods.

Coryphaeus

Cadmus, I pity you. Your daughter's son
has died as he deserved, and yet his death
bears hard on you.

[*At this point there is a break in the manuscript of nearly fifty lines.
The following speeches of Agave and Coryphaeus and the first part of
Dionysus' speech have been conjecturally reconstructed from fragments and
later material which made use of the Bacchae. Lines which can plausibly
be assigned to the lacuna are otherwise not indicated. My own inventions
are designed, not to complete the speeches, but to effect a transition between the fragments, and are bracketed. For fuller comment, see the Appendix.*—TRANS.]

Agave

          O Father, now you can see
how everything has changed. I am in anguish now,
tormented, who walked in triumph minutes past,
exulting in my kill. And that prize I carried home
with such pride was my own curse. Upon these hands
I bear the curse of my son's blood. How then
with these accursed hands may I touch his body?
How can I, accursed with such a curse, hold him
to my breast? O gods, what dirge can I sing
[that there might be] a dirge [for every]
broken limb?

.   .   .   .

          Where is a shroud to cover up his corpse?
O my child, what hands will give you proper care
unless with my own hands I lift my curse?

*(She lifts up one of Pentheus' limbs and asks the help of Cadmus
in piecing the body together. She mourns each piece separate-
ly before replacing it on the bier. See Appendix.)*

Come, Father. We must restore his head
to this unhappy boy. As best we can, we shall make
him whole again.

        —O dearest, dearest face!
Pretty boyish mouth! Now with this veil
I shroud your head, gathering with loving care
these mangled bloody limbs, this flesh I brought
to birth

. . . .

Coryphaeus

Let this scene teach those [who see these things:
Dionysus is the son] of Zeus.

(Above the palace Dionysus appears in epiphany.)

Dionysus

        [I am Dionysus,
the son of Zeus, returned to Thebes, revealed,
a god to men.] But the men [of Thebes] blasphemed me.
They slandered me; they said I came of mortal man,
and not content with speaking blasphemies,
[they dared to threaten my person with violence.]
These crimes this people whom I cherished well
did from malice to their benefactor. Therefore,
I now disclose the sufferings in store for them.
Like [enemies], they shall be driven from this city
to other lands; there, submitting to the yoke
of slavery, they shall wear out wretched lives,
captives of war, enduring much indignity.

(He turns to the corpse of Pentheus.)

This man has found the death which he deserved,
torn to pieces among the jagged rocks.
You are my witnesses: he came with outrage;

he attempted to chain my hands, abusing me
[and doing what he should least of all have done.]
And therefore he has rightly perished by the hands
of those who should the least of all have murdered him.
What he suffers, he suffers justly.

Upon you,
Agave, and on your sisters I pronounce this doom:
you shall leave this city in expiation
of the murder you have done. You are unclean,
and it would be a sacrilege that murderers
should remain at peace beside the graves [of those
whom they have killed].

(*He turns to Cadmus.*)

.   .   .   .

Next I shall disclose the trials
which await this man. You, Cadmus, shall be changed   1330
to a serpent, and your wife, the child of Ares,
immortal Harmonia, shall undergo your doom,
a serpent too. With her, it is your fate
to go a journey in a car drawn on by oxen,
leading behind you a great barbarian host.
For thus decrees the oracle of Zeus.
With a host so huge its numbers cannot be counted,   1335
you shall ravage many cities; but when your army
plunders the shrine of Apollo, its homecoming
shall be perilous and hard. Yet in the end
the god Ares shall save Harmonia and you
and bring you both to live among the blest.

So say I, born of no mortal father,   1340
Dionysus, true son of Zeus. If then,
when you would not, you had muzzled your madness,
you should have an ally now in the son of Zeus.

Cadmus

We implore you, Dionysus. We have done wrong.

Dionysus

Too late. When there was time, you did not know me.   1345

Cadmus

We have learned. But your sentence is too harsh.

Dionysus

I am a god. I was blasphemed by you.

Cadmus

Gods should be exempt from human passions.

Dionysus

Long ago my father Zeus ordained these things.

Agave

It is fated, Father. We must go.

Dionysus

                              Why then delay?   1350
For you must go.

Cadmus

                         Child, to what a dreadful end
have we all come, you and your wretched sisters
and my unhappy self. An old man, I must go
to live a stranger among barbarian peoples, doomed   1355
to lead against Hellas a motley foreign army.
Transformed to serpents, I and my wife,
Harmonia, the child of Ares, we must captain
spearsmen against the tombs and shrines of Hellas.
Never shall my sufferings end; not even   1360
over Acheron shall I have peace.

Agave (embracing Cadmus)

                         O Father,
to be banished, to live without you!

Cadmus

                                Poor child,

like a white swan warding its weak old father,   1365

why do you clasp those white arms about my neck?

Agave

But banished! Where shall I go?

Cadmus

                         I do not know,

my child. Your father can no longer help you.

Agave

Farewell, my home! City, farewell.

O bridal bed, banished I go,   1370

in misery, I leave you now.

Cadmus

Go, poor child, seek shelter in Aristaeus' house.

Agave

I pity you, Father.

Cadmus

                  And I pity you, my child,

and I grieve for your poor sisters. I pity them.

Agave

Terribly has Dionysus brought   1375

disaster down upon this house.

Dionysus

I was terribly blasphemed,

my name dishonored in Thebes.

Agave

Farewell, Father.

Cadmus

Farewell to you, unhappy child.
Fare well. But you shall find your faring hard.   1380

(*Exit Cadmus.*)

Agave

Lead me, guides, where my sisters wait,
poor sisters of my exile. Let me go
where I shall never see Cithaeron more,   1385
where that accursed hill may not see me,
where I shall find no trace of thyrsus!
That I leave to other Bacchae.

(*Exit Agave with attendants.*)

Chorus

The gods have many shapes.
The gods bring many things
to their accomplishment.
And what was most expected   1390
has not been accomplished.
But god has found his way
for what no man expected.
So ends the play.

APPENDIX TO *THE BACCHAE*

APPENDIX

Reconstruction of the long lacuna (l. 1329) can never be more than conjectural; but it can at least be that. I have attempted it in the conviction that its presence seriously hinders any possible production of the play.

The contents of the lacuna are, at least in outline, tolerably clear. A third-century rhetorician, Apsines, describes the speech of Agave, how she arouses pity by "picking up in her hands each one of her son's limbs and mourning it individually" (see Apsines *Rhet. Gr.* [ed.Walz], ix. 587). Then, according to the hypothesis of the play, Dionysus appears and addresses all, and foretells the future of each one in turn. The manuscript picks up the speech of Dionysus at line 1330 with an account, virtually complete, of the fate of Cadmus. Against this framework, scholars have been able to place a large number of Euripidean lines from the *Christus Patiens*, a twelfth-century cento, made up of lines from at least seven Euripidean plays. The bulk of the lines which fill the lacuna in my translation come from the *C.P.* Some of them are almost certain; others less so; but together they go a long way toward rounding out the gap. Thorough discussion of the lacuna problem may be found in the commentary on line 1329 in Dodds's edition of *The Bacchae*.

The order of my lines is as follows: beginning, *Bacchae*, l. 1329; *C.P.* ll. 1011, 1311, 1312, 1313, 1256, 1122, 1123; Schol. in Ar. Plut. l. 907; *C.P.* ll. 1466, 1467, 1468, 1469, 1470; Pap. Ant. 24 (*Antinoopolis Pap.* I, ed. C. H. Roberts, 1951) and *C.P.* l. 1472. The speech of Coryphaeus: pap. frag. (cf. Dodds, App. I). The speech of Dionysus: *C.P.* ll. 1360–62, 1665–66, 1668–69, 1678–80, 300; Lucian, *Pisc.* 2; *C.P.* ll. 1692, 1664, 1663, 1667, 1674–78, 1690.

ALCESTIS

Translated by Richmond Lattimore

INTRODUCTION

Alcestis, the earliest extant play of Euripides, was produced in 438 B.C. and won second prize.

The given story was that Admetus, king of Thessaly, could avoid his fated early death if someone else would volunteer to die in his place. Alcestis, his wife, did so; no other would. But Heracles, the friend of Admetus, fought the spirit of Death and took Alcestis away from him and restored her to her husband. The story had been told by Phrynichus, the early-fifth-century tragedian, in a lost satyr-play.

Euripides could have made the main point of his action the heroism of the wife. He does, of course, acknowledge and celebrate this, but the story is really the story of Admetus, the man who let his wife die in his place, his struggle with the unstated fact and final acknowledgment of it. This comes just before her restoration and makes more plausible the miraculous favor shown him by his friends, Apollo and Heracles, as a reward for justice and hospitality. Miracles apart, the play can be read as the study of a good but untried and unready man facing the overwhelming fact of death.

A tragedy with a happy ending, almost a tragedy in reverse, *Alcestis* occupied fourth place in its series and is thus a substitute for the cheerful, ribald satyr-play which customarily concluded the tragic trilogy. It is probably unwise to try to see any elements of satyr-play in it, except for the temporary drunkenness of Heracles, which, as far as it goes, is in the manner of satyr-play and comedy. The choral odes are exceptionally sincere, and throughout the play Euripides' unpretentious style is at its best.

NOTE

The text followed is Murray's Oxford text, and his line numbers, which are standard, have been used, except that different readings have been adopted which affect the translation of the following lines: 50, 124, 223, 943, 1140, 1153.

CHARACTERS

Apollo

Death

Chorus of citizens of Pherae

Maid, attendant of Alcestis

Alcestis, wife of Admetus

Admetus of Pherae, king of Thessaly

Boy (Eumelus), son of Admetus and Alcestis

Heracles

Pheres, father of Admetus

Servant of Admetus

Girl, daughter of Admetus and Alcestis (silent character)

Servants (silent)

ALCESTIS

SCENE: *Pherae, in Thessaly, before the house of Admetus. The front door*
of the house, or palace, is the center of the backdrop.

(*Enter Apollo from the house, armed with a bow.*)
Apollo

House of Admetus, in which I, god though I am,
had patience to accept the table of the serfs!
Zeus was the cause. Zeus killed my son, Asclepius,
and drove the bolt of the hot lightning through his chest.
I, in my anger for this, killed the Cyclopes,   5
smiths of Zeus's fire, for which my father made me serve
a mortal man, in penance for my misdoings.
I came to this country, tended the oxen of this host
and friend, Admetus, son of Pheres. I have kept
his house from danger, cheated the Fates to save his life   10
until this day, for he revered my sacred rights
sacredly, and the fatal goddesses allowed
Admetus to escape the moment of his death
by giving the lower powers someone else to die
instead of him. He tried his loved ones all in turn,   15
father and aged mother who had given him birth,
and found not one, except his wife, who would consent
to die for him, and not see daylight any more.
She is in the house now, gathered in his arms and held
at the breaking point of life, because the destiny marks   20
this for her day of death and taking leave of life.
The stain of death in the house must not be on me. I
step therefore from these chambers dearest to my love.
And here is Death himself, I see him coming, Death
who dedicates the dying, who will lead her down   25
to the house of Hades. He has come on time. He has
been watching for this day on which her death falls due.

(Enter Death, armed with a sword, from the wing. He sees
Apollo suddenly and shows surprise.)

Death

Ah!
You at this house, Phoebus? Why do you haunt
the place. It is unfair to take for your own   30
and spoil the death-spirits' privileges.
Was it not enough, then, that you blocked the death
of Admetus, and overthrew the Fates
by a shabby wrestler's trick? And now
your bow hand is armed to guard her too,   35
Alcestis, Pelias' daughter, though she
promised her life for her husband's.

Apollo

Never fear. I have nothing but justice and fair words for you.

Death

If you mean fairly, what are you doing with a bow?

Apollo

It is my custom to carry it with me all the time.   40

Death

It is your custom to help this house more than you ought.

Apollo

But he is my friend, and his misfortunes trouble me.

Death

You mean to take her body, too, away from me?

Apollo

I never took *his* body away from you by force.

Death

How is it, then, that he is above ground, not below?   45

Apollo

He gave his wife instead, and you have come for her now.

Death

I have. And I shall take her down where the dead are.

Apollo

Take her and go. I am not sure you will listen to me.

Death

Tell me to kill whom I must kill. Such are my orders.

Apollo

No, only to put their death off. They must die in the end.   50

Death

I understand what you would say and what you want.

Apollo

Is there any way, then, for Alcestis to grow old?

Death

There is not. I insist on enjoying my rights too.

Apollo

You would not take more than one life, in any case.

Death

My privilege means more to me when they die young.   55

Apollo

If she dies old, she will have a lavish burial.

Death

What you propose, Phoebus, is to favor the rich.

Apollo

What is this? Have you unrecognized talents for debate?

Death

Those who could afford to buy a late death would buy it then.

Apollo

I see. Are you determined not to do this for me?   60

Death

I will not do it. And you know my character.

Apollo

I know it: hateful to mankind, loathed by the gods.

Death

You cannot always have your way where you should not.

Apollo

For all your brute ferocity you shall be stopped.
The man to do it is on the way to Pheres' house   65
now, on an errand from Eurystheus, sent to steal
a team of horses from the wintry lands of Thrace.
He shall be entertained here in Admetus' house
and he shall take the woman away from you by force,
nor will you have our gratitude, but you shall still   70
be forced to do it, and to have my hate beside.

Death

Much talk. Talking will win you nothing. All the same,
the woman goes with me to Hades' house. I go
to take her now, and dedicate her with my sword,
for all whose hair is cut in consecration   75
by this blade's edge are devoted to the gods below.

(*Death enters the house. Apollo leaves by the wing. The
Chorus enters and forms a group before the gates.*)

Chorus

It is quiet by the palace. What does it mean?
Why is the house of Admetus so still?
Is there none here of his family, none
who can tell us whether the queen is dead   80
and therefore to be mourned? Or does Pelias'
daughter Alcestis live still, still look
on daylight, she who in my mind appears
noble beyond
all women beside in a wife's duty?   85

(*Here they speak individually, not as a group.*)

First Citizen

Does someone hear anything?

The sound a hand's stroke would make,
or outcry, as if something were done
and over?

Second Citizen

　　　　No. And there is no servant stationed
at the outer gates. O Paean,　　　　　　　　　　　90
healer, might you show in light
to still the storm of disaster.

Third Citizen

They would not be silent if she were dead.

Fourth Citizen

No, she is gone.

Fifth Citizen

They have not taken her yet from the house.

Sixth Citizen

So sure? I know nothing. Why are you certain?　　　95
And how could Admetus have buried his wife
with none by, and she so splendid?

Seventh Citizen

Here at the gates I do not see
the lustral spring water, approved
by custom for a house of death.　　　　　　　　　　100

Eighth Citizen

Nor are there cut locks of hair at the forecourts
hanging, such as the stroke of sorrow
for the dead makes. I can hear no beating
of the hands of young women.

Ninth Citizen

Yet this is the day appointed.　　　　　　　　　　105

Tenth Citizen

What do you mean? Speak.

Ninth Citizen

On which she must pass to the world below.

Eleventh Citizen

You touch me deep, my heart, where it hurts.

Twelfth Citizen

Yes. He who from the first has claimed to be called
a good man himself   110
must grieve when good men are afflicted.

(*Henceforward all the Chorus together.*)

Sailing the long sea, there is
not any place on earth
you could win, not Lycia,
not the unwatered sands called   115
of Ammon, not
thus to approach and redeem the life
of this unhappy woman. Her fate shows
steep and near. There is no god's hearth
I know you could reach and by sacrifice   120
avail to save.

There was only one. If the eyes
of Phoebus' son were opened
still, if he could have come
and left the dark chambers,   125
the gates of Hades.
He upraised those who were stricken
down, until from the hand of God
the flown bolt of thunder hit him.
Where is there any hope for life   130
left for me any longer?

For all has been done that can be done by our kings now,
and there on all the gods' altars
are blood sacrifices dripping in full,
but no healing comes for the evil.   135

(Enter a maid from the house.)

Chorus

But here is a serving woman coming from the house.
The tears break from her. What will she say has taken place?
We must, of course, forgive your sorrow if something
has happened to your masters. We should like to know
whether the queen is dead or if she is still alive.   140

Maid

I could tell you that she is still alive or that she is dead.

Chorus

How could a person both be dead and live and see?

Maid

It has felled her, and the life is breaking from her now.

Chorus

Such a husband, to lose such a wife. I pity you.

Maid

The master does not see it and he will not see it   145
until it happens.

Chorus

There is no hope left she will live?

Maid

None. This is the day of destiny. It is too strong.

Chorus

Surely, he must be doing all he can for her.

Maid

All is prepared so he can bury her in style.

Chorus

Let her be sure, at least, that as she dies, there dies   150
the noblest woman underneath the sun, by far.

Maid

Noblest? Of course the noblest, who will argue that?
What shall the wife be who surpasses her? And how

could any woman show that she loves her husband more
than herself better than by consent to die for him?   155
But all the city knows that well. You shall be told
now how she acted in the house, and be amazed
to hear. For when she understood the fatal day
was come, she bathed her white body with water drawn
from running streams, then opened the cedar chest and took   160
her clothes out, and dressed in all her finery
and stood before the Spirit in the Hearth, and prayed:
"Mistress, since I am going down beneath the ground,
I kneel before you in this last of all my prayers.
Take care of my children for me. Give the little girl   165
a husband; give the little boy a generous wife;
and do not let my children die like me, who gave
them birth, untimely. Let them live a happy life
through to the end and prosper here in their own land."
Afterward she approached the altars, all that stand   170
in the house of Admetus, made her prayers, and decked them all
with fresh sprays torn from living myrtle. And she wept
not at all, made no outcry. The advancing doom
made no change in the color and beauty of her face.
But then, in their room, she threw herself upon the bed,   175
and there she did cry, there she spoke: "O marriage bed,
it was here that I undressed my maidenhood and gave
myself up to this husband for whose sake I die.
Goodbye. I hold no grudge. But you have been my death
and mine alone. I could not bear to play him false.   180
I die. Some other woman will possess you now.
She will not be better, but she might be happier."
She fell on the bed and kissed it. All the coverings
were drenched in the unchecked outpouring of her tears;
but after much crying, when all her tears were shed,   185
she rolled from the couch and walked away with eyes cast down,
began to leave the room, but turned and turned again
to fling herself once more upon the bed. Meanwhile
the children clung upon their mother's dress, and cried,

until she gathered them into her arms, and kissed   190
first one and then the other, as in death's farewell.
And all the servants in the house were crying now
in sorrow for their mistress. Then she gave her hand
to each, and each one took it, there was none so mean
in station that she did not stop and talk with him.   195
This is what Admetus and the house are losing. Had
he died, he would have lost her, but in this escape
he will keep the pain. It will not ever go away.

Chorus

Admetus surely must be grieving over this
when such a wife must be taken away from him.   200

Maid

Oh yes, he is crying. He holds his wife close in his arms,
imploring her not to forsake him. What he wants
is impossible. She is dying. The sickness fades her now.
She has gone slack, just an inert weight on the arm.
Still, though so little breath of life is left in her,   205
she wants to look once more upon the light of the sun,
since this will be the last time of all, and never again.
She must see the sun's shining circle yet one more time.
Now I must go announce your presence. It is not
everyone who bears so much good will toward our kings   210
as to stand by ready to help in their distress.
But you have been my master's friends since long ago.

                                                            (*Exit.*)

Chorus

O Zeus, Zeus, what way out of this evil
is there, what escape from this
which is happening to our princes?
A way, any way? Must I cut short my hair   215
for grief, put upon me the black
costume that means mourning?
We must, friends, clearly we must; yet still

let us pray to the gods. The gods
have power beyond all power elsewhere.

Paean, my lord,   220
Apollo, make some way of escape for Admetus.
Grant it, oh grant it. Once you found
rescue in him. Be now
in turn his redeemer from death.
Oppose bloodthirsty Hades.   225

Admetus,
O son of Pheres, what a loss
to suffer, when such a wife goes.
A man could cut his throat for this, for this
and less he could bind the noose upon his neck
and hang himself. For this is   230
not only dear, but dearest of all,
this wife you will see dead
on this day before you.

> (*Alcestis is carried from the house on a litter, supported by*
> *Admetus and followed by her children and*
> *servants of the household.*)

But see, see,
she is coming out of the house and her husband is with her.
Cry out aloud, mourn, you land
of Pherae for the bravest   235
of wives fading in sickness and doomed
to the Death God of the world below.

I will never again say that marriage brings
more pleasure than pain. I judge by what
I have known in the past, and by seeing now   240
what happens to our king, who is losing a wife
brave beyond all others, and must live a life
that will be no life for the rest of time.

Alcestis

Sun, and light of the day,
O turning wheel of the sky, clouds that fly.   245

Admetus

The sun sees you and me, two people suffering,
who never hurt the gods so they should make you die.

Alcestis

My land, and palace arching my land,
and marriage chambers of Iolcus, my own country.

Admetus

Raise yourself, my Alcestis, do not leave me now.   250
I implore the gods to pity you. They have the power.

Alcestis

I see him there at the oars of his little boat in the lake,
the ferryman of the dead,
Charon, with his hand upon the oar,
and he calls me now: "What keeps you?   255
Hurry, you hold us back." He is urging me on
in angry impatience.

Admetus

The crossing you speak of is a bitter one for me;
ill starred; it is unfair we should be treated so.

Alcestis

Somebody has me, somebody takes me away, do you see,
don't you see, to the courts   260
of dead men. He frowns from under dark
brows. He has wings. It is Death.
Let me go, what are you doing, let go.

                                        Such is the road
most wretched I have to walk.

Admetus

Sorrow for all who love you, most of all for me
and for the children. All of us share in this grief.   265

Alcestis

Let me go now, let me down,
flat. I have no strength to stand.

Death is close to me.
The darkness creeps over my eyes. O children,
my children, you have no mother now,
not any longer. Daylight is yours,
my children. Look on it and be happy.

Admetus

Ah, a bitter word for me to hear,
heavier than any death of my own.
Before the gods, do not be so harsh
as to leave me, leave your children forlorn.
No, up, and fight it.
There would be nothing left of me if you died.
All rests in you, our life, our not
having life. Your love is our worship.

Alcestis

Admetus, you can see how it is with me. Therefore,
I wish to have some words with you before I die.
I put you first, and at the price of my own life
made certain you would live and see the daylight. So
I die, who did not have to die, because of you.
I could have taken any man in Thessaly
I wished and lived in queenly state here in this house.
But since I did not wish to live bereft of you
and with our children fatherless, I did not spare
my youth, although I had so much to live for. Yet
your father, and the mother who bore you, gave you up,
though they had reached an age when it was good to die
and good to save their son and end it honorably.
You were their only one, and they had no more hope
of having other children if you died. That way
I would be living and you would live the rest of our time,
and you would not be alone and mourning for your wife
and tending motherless children. No, but it must be
that some god has so wrought that things shall be this way.
So be it. But swear now to do, in recompense,

270

275

280

285

290

295

what I shall ask you—not enough, oh, never enough,   300
since nothing is enough to make up for a life,
but fair, and you yourself will say so, since you love
these children as much as I do; or at least you should.
Keep them as masters in my house, and do not marry
again and give our children to a stepmother   305
who will not be so kind as I, who will be jealous
and raise her hand to your children and mine. Oh no,
do not do that, do not. That is my charge to you.
For the new-come stepmother hates the children born
to a first wife, no viper could be deadlier.   310
The little boy has his father for a tower of strength.
[He can talk with him and be spoken to in turn.]
But you, my darling, what will your girlhood be like,
how will your father's new wife like you? She must not
make shameful stories up about you, and contrive   315
to spoil your chance of marriage in the blush of youth,
because your mother will not be there to help you
when you are married, not be there to give you strength
when your babies are born, when only a mother's help will do.
For I must die. It will not be tomorrow, not   320
the next day, or this month, the horrible thing will come,
but now, at once, I shall be counted among the dead.
Goodbye, be happy, both of you. And you, my husband,
can boast the bride you took made you the bravest wife,
and you, children, can say, too, that your mother was brave.   325

Chorus

Fear nothing; for I dare to speak for him. He will
do all you ask. If he does not, the fault is his.

Admetus

It shall be so, it shall be, do not fear, since you
were mine in life, you still shall be my bride in death
and you alone, no other girl in Thessaly   330
shall ever be called wife of Admetus in your place.
There is none such, none so marked out in pride of birth

nor beauty's brilliance, nor in anything else. I have
these children, they are enough; I only pray the gods
grant me the bliss to keep them as we could not keep you.   335
I shall go into mourning for you, not for just
a year, but all my life while it still lasts, my dear,
and hate the woman who gave me birth always, detest
my father. These were called my own people. They were not.
You gave what was your own and dear to buy my life   340
and saved me. Am I not to lead a mourning life
when I have lost a wife like you? I shall make an end
of revelry and entertainment in my house,
the flowers and the music that were found here once.
No, I shall never touch the lutestrings ever again   345
nor have the heart to play music upon the flute
of Libya, for you took my joy in life with you.
I shall have the skilled hand of an artificer
make me an image of you to set in my room,
pay my devotions to it, hold it in my arms   350
and speak your name, and clasp it close against my heart,
and think I hold my wife again, though I do not,
cold consolation, I know it, and yet even so
I might drain the weight of sorrow. You could come
to see me in my dreams and comfort me. For they   355
who love find a time's sweetness in the visions of night.
Had I the lips of Orpheus and his melody
to charm the maiden daughter of Demeter and
her lord, and by my singing win you back from death,
I would have gone beneath the earth, and not the hound   360
of Pluto could have stayed me, not the ferryman
of ghosts, Charon at his oar. I would have brought you back
to life. Wait for me, then, in that place, till I die,
and make ready the room where you will live with me,
for I shall have them bury me in the same chest   365
as you, and lay me at your side, so that my heart
shall be against your heart, and never, even in death
shall I go from you. You alone were true to me.

Chorus

 And I, because I am your friend and you
 are mine, shall help you bear this sorrow, as I should.   370

Alcestis

 Children, you now have heard your father promise me
 that he will never marry again and not inflict
 a new wife on you, but will keep my memory.

Admetus

 I promise. I will keep my promise to the end.

Alcestis

 On this condition, take the children. They are yours.   375

Admetus

 I take them, a dear gift from a dear hand.

Alcestis

              And now
 you must be our children's mother, too, instead of me.

Admetus

 I must be such, since they will no longer have you.

Alcestis

 O children, this was my time to live, and I must go.

Admetus

 Ah me, what shall I do without you all alone.   380

Alcestis

 Time will soften it. The dead count for nothing at all.

Admetus

 Oh, take me with you, for God's love, take me there too.

Alcestis

 No, I am dying in your place. That is enough.

Admetus

 O God, what a wife you are taking away from me.

Alcestis

It is true. My eyes darken and the heaviness comes.   385

Admetus

But I am lost, dear, if you leave me.

Alcestis

There is no use
in talking to me any more. I am not there.

Admetus

No, lift your head up, do not leave your children thus.

Alcestis

I do not want to, but it is goodbye, children.

Admetus

Look at them, oh look at them.

Alcestis

No. There is nothing more.   390

Admetus

Are you really leaving us?

Alcestis

Goodbye.

Admetus

Oh, I am lost.

Chorus

It is over now. Admetus' wife is gone from us.

Boy

O wicked fortune. Mother has gone down there,
father, she is not here with us
in the sunshine any more.   395
She was cruel and went away
and left me to live all alone.
Look at her eyes, look at her hands, so still.
Hear me, mother, listen to me, oh please,   400
listen, it is I, mother,
I your little one lean and kiss
your lips, and cry out to you.

Admetus

She does not see, she does not hear you. You and I
both have a hard and heavy load to carry now.   405

Boy

Father, I am too small to be left alone
by the mother I loved so much. Oh,
it is hard for me to bear
all this that is happening,
and you, little sister, suffer   410
with me too. Oh, father,
your marriage was empty, empty, she did not live
to grow old with you.
She died too soon. Mother, with you gone away,
the whole house is ruined.   415

(*Alcestis is carried into the house, followed
by children and servants.*)

Chorus

Admetus, you must stand up to misfortune now.
You are not the first, and not the last of humankind
to lose a good wife. Therefore, you must understand
death is an obligation claimed from all of us.

Admetus

I understand it. And this evil which has struck   420
was no surprise. I knew about it long ago,
and knowledge was hard. But now, since we must bury our dead,
stay with me and stand by me, chant responsively
the hymn of the unsacrificed-to god below.
To all Thessalians over whom my rule extends   425
I ordain a public mourning for my wife, to be
observed with shaving of the head and with black robes.
The horses that you drive in chariots and those
you ride single shall have their manes cut short with steel,
and there shall be no sound of flutes within the city,   430
no sound of lyres, until twelve moons have filled and gone;
for I shall never bury any dearer dead

than she, nor any who loved me better. She deserves
my thanks. She died for me, which no one else would do.

(Exit into the house.)

Chorus

O daughter of Pelias   435
my wish for you is a happy life
in the sunless chambers of Hades.
Now let the dark-haired lord of Death himself, and the old man,
who sits at the steering oar   440
and ferries the corpses,
know that you are the bravest of wives, by far,
ever conveyed across the tarn
of Acheron in the rowboat.

Much shall be sung of you   445
by the men of music to the seven-strung mountain
lyre-shell, and in poems that have no music,
in Sparta when the season turns and the month Carneian
comes back, and the moon
rides all the night;   450
in Athens also, the shining and rich.
Such is the theme of song you left
in death, for the poets.

Oh that it were in my power   455
and that I had strength to bring you
back to light from the dark of death
with oars on the sunken river.
For you, O dearest among women, you only   460
had the hard courage
to give your life for your husband's and save
him from death. May the dust lie light
upon you, my lady. And should he now take
a new wife to his bed, he will win my horror and hatred,
mine, and your children's hatred too.   465

His mother would not endure
to have her body hidden in the ground

for him, nor the aged father.
He was theirs, but they had not courage to save him.
Oh shame, for the gray was upon them. 470
But you, in the pride
of youth, died for him and left the daylight.
May it only be mine to win
such wedded love as hers from a wife; for this
is given seldom to mortals; but were my wife such, I would
have her
with me unhurt through her lifetime. 475

(Enter Heracles from the road, travel-stained.)

Heracles

My friends, people of Pherae and the villages
hereby, tell me, shall I find Admetus at home?

Chorus

Yes, Heracles, the son of Pheres is in the house.
But tell us, what is the errand that brings you here
to Thessaly and the city of Pherae once again? 480

Heracles

I have a piece of work to do for Eurystheus
of Tiryns.

Chorus

Where does it take you? On what far journey?

Heracles

To Thrace, to take home Diomedes' chariot.

Chorus

How can you? Do you know the man you are to meet?

Heracles

No. I have never been where the Bistones live. 485

Chorus

You cannot master his horses. Not without a fight.

Heracles

It is my work, and I cannot refuse.

Chorus

        You must
kill him before you come back; or be killed and stay.

Heracles

If I must fight, it will not be for the first time.

Chorus

What good will it do you if you overpower their master?   490

Heracles

I will take the horses home to Tiryns and its king.

Chorus

It is not easy to put a bridle on their jaws.

Heracles

Easy enough, unless their nostrils are snorting fire.

Chorus

Not that, but they have teeth that tear a man apart.

Heracles

Oh no! Mountain beasts, not horses, feed like that.   495

Chorus

But you can see their mangers. They are caked with blood.

Heracles

And the man who raises them? Whose son does he claim he is?

Chorus

Ares'. And he is lord of the golden shield of Thrace.

Heracles

It sounds like my life and the kind of work I do.
It is a hard and steep way always that I go,   500
having to fight one after another all the sons
the war god ever got him, with Lycaon first,
again with Cycnus, and now here is a third fight
that I must have with the master of these horses. So—

I am Alcmene's son, and the man does not live   505
who will see me break before my enemy's attack.

Chorus

Here is the monarch of our country coming
from the house himself, Admetus.

(*Enter Admetus.*)

Admetus

Welcome and happiness
to you, O scion of Perseus' blood and child of Zeus.

Heracles

Happiness to you likewise, lord of Thessaly,   510
Admetus.

Admetus

I could wish it. I know you mean well.

Heracles

What is the matter? Why is there mourning and cut hair?

Admetus

There is one dead here whom I must bury today.

Heracles

Not one of your children! I pray God shield them from that.

Admetus

Not they. My children are well and living in their house.   515

Heracles

If it is your father who is gone, his time was ripe.

Admetus

No, he is still there, Heracles. My mother, too.

Heracles

Surely you have not lost your wife, Alcestis.

Admetus

Yes
and no. There are two ways that I could answer that.

Heracles

Did you say that she is dead or that she is still alive?   520

Admetus

She is, but she is gone away. It troubles me.

Heracles

I still do not know what you mean. You are being obscure.

Admetus

You know about her and what must happen, do you not?

Heracles

I know that she has undertaken to die for you.

Admetus

How can she really live, then, when she has promised that?   525

Heracles

Ah, do not mourn her before she dies. Wait for the time.

Admetus

The point of death is death, and the dead are lost and gone.

Heracles

Being and nonbeing are considered different things.

Admetus

That is your opinion, Heracles. It is not mine.

Heracles

Well, but whose is the mourning now? Is it in the family?   530

Admetus

A woman. We were speaking of a woman, were we not?

Heracles

Was she a blood relative or someone from outside?

Admetus

No relation by blood, but she meant much to us.

Heracles

How does it happen that she died here in your house?

Admetus

She lost her father and came here to live with us.   535

Heracles

I am sorry,
Admetus. I wish I had found you in a happier state.

Admetus

Why do you say that? What do you mean to do?

Heracles

I mean
to go on, and stay with another of my friends.

Admetus

No, my lord, no. The evil must not come to that.

Heracles

The friend who stays with friends in mourning is in the way.   540

Admetus

The dead are dead. Go on in.

Heracles

No. It is always wrong
for guests to revel in a house where others mourn.

Admetus

There are separate guest chambers. We can take you there.

Heracles

Let me go, and I will thank you a thousand times.

Admetus

You shall not go to stay with any other man.   545
You there: open the guest rooms which are across the court
from the house, and tell the people who are there to provide
plenty to eat, and make sure that you close the doors

facing the inside court. It is not right for guests
to have their pleasures interrupted by sounds of grief.   550

(Heracles is ushered inside.)

Chorus

Admetus, are you crazy? What are you thinking of
to entertain guests in a situation like this?

Admetus

And if I had driven from my city and my house
the guest and friend who came to me, would you have approved
of me more? Wrong. My misery would still have been   555
as great, and I should be inhospitable too,
and there would be one more misfortune added to those
I have, if my house is called unfriendly to its friends.
For this man is my best friend, and he is my host
whenever I go to Argos, which is a thirsty place.   560

Chorus

Yes, but then why did you hide what is happening here
if this visitor is, as you say, your best friend?

Admetus

He would not have been willing to come inside my house
if he had known what trouble I was in. I know.
There are some will think I show no sense in doing this.   565
They will not like it. But my house does not know how
to push its friends away and not treat them as it should.

(He goes inside.)

Chorus

O liberal and forever free-handed house of this man,
the Pythian himself, lyric Apollo,   570
was pleased to live with you
and had patience upon your lands
to work as a shepherd,
and on the hill-folds and the slopes   575
piped to the pasturing of your flocks
in their season of mating.

And even dappled lynxes for delight in his melody
joined him as shepherds. From the cleft of Othrys descended   580
a red troop of lions,
and there, Phoebus, to your lyre's strain
there danced the bright-coated
fawn, adventuring from the deep   585
bearded pines, lightfooted for joy
in your song, in its kindness.

Therefore, your house is beyond
all others for wealth of flocks by the sweet waters
of Lake Boebias. For spread of cornland   590
and pasturing range its boundary stands
only there where the sun
stalls his horses in dark air by the Molossians.
Eastward he sways all to the harborless   595
Pelian coast on the Aegaean main.

Now he has spread wide his doors
and taken the guest in, when his eyes were wet
and he wept still for a beloved wife who died
in the house so lately. The noble strain   600
comes out, in respect for others.
All that wisdom means is there in the noble. I stand
in awe, and good hope has come again to my heart
that for this godly man the end will be good.   605

(Enter Admetus from the house, followed by
servants with a covered litter.)

Admetus

Gentlemen of Pherae, I am grateful for your company.
My men are bearing to the burning place and grave
our dead, who now has all the state which is her due.
Will you then, as the custom is among us, say
farewell to the dead as she goes forth for the last time?   610

Chorus

Yes, but I see your father coming now. He walks

« 289 »

as old men do, and followers carry in their hands
gifts for your wife, to adorn her in the underworld.

(Enter Pheres, attended, from outside.)

Pheres

I have come to bear your sorrows with you, son. I know,
nobody will dispute it, you have lost a wife   615
both good and modest in her ways. Nevertheless,
you have to bear it, even though it is hard to bear.
Accept these gifts to deck her body, bury them
with her. Oh yes, she well deserves honor in death.
She died to save your life, my son. She would not let   620
me be a childless old man, would not let me waste
away in sorrowful age deprived of you. Thereby,
daring this generous action, she has made the life
of all women become a thing of better repute
than it was.

O you who saved him, you who raised us up   625
when we were fallen, farewell, even in Hades' house
may good befall you.

I say people ought to marry women
like this. Otherwise, better not to marry at all.

Admetus

I never invited you to come and see her buried,
nor do I count your company as that of a friend.   630
She shall not wear anything that you bring her.
She needs nothing from you to be buried in. Your time
to share my sorrow was when I was about to die.
But you stood out of the way and let youth take my place
in death, though you were old. Will you cry for her now?   635
It cannot be that my body ever came from you,
nor did the woman who claims she bore me and is called
my mother give me birth. I was got from some slave
and surreptitiously put to your wife to nurse.
You show it. Your nature in the crisis has come out.   640
I do not count myself as any child of yours.

Oh, you outpass the cowardice of all the world,
you at your age, come to the very last step of life
and would not, dared not, die for your own child. Oh, no,
you let this woman, married into our family,   645
do it instead, and therefore it is right for me
to call her all the father and mother that I have.
And yet you two should honorably have striven for
the right of dying for your child. The time of life
you had left for your living was short, in any case,   650
and she and I would still be living out our time
and I should not be hurt and grieving over her.
And yet, all that a man could have to bless his life
you have had. You had your youth in kingship. There was I
your son, ready to take it over, keep your house   655
in order, so you had no childless death to fear,
with the house left to be torn apart by other claims.
You cannot justify your leaving me to death
on grounds that I disrespected your old age. Always I
showed all consideration. See what thanks I get   660
from you and from the woman who gave me birth. Go on,
get you other children, you cannot do it too soon,
who will look after your old age, and lay you out
when you are dead, and see you buried properly.
I will not do it. This hand will never bury you.   665
I am dead as far as you are concerned, and if, because
I found another savior, I still look on the sun,
I count myself that person's child and fond support.
It is meaningless, the way the old men pray for death
and complain of age and the long time they have to live.   670
Let death only come close, not one of them still wants
to die. Their age is not a burden any more.

Chorus

Stop, stop. We have trouble enough already, child.
You will exasperate your father with this talk.

Pheres

Big words, son. Who do you think you are cursing out   675
like this? Some Lydian slave, some Phrygian that you bought?
I am a free Thessalian noble, nobly born
from a Thessalian. Are you forgetting that? You go
too far with your high-handedness. You volley brash
words at me, and fail to hit me, and then run away.   680
I gave you life, and made you master of my house,
and raised you. I am not obliged to die for you.
I do not acknowledge any tradition among us
that fathers should die for their sons. That is not Greek.
Your natural right is to find your own happiness   685
or unhappiness. All you deserve from me, you have.
You are lord of many. I have wide estates of land
to leave you, just as my father left them to me.
What harm have I done you then? What am I taking away
from you? Do not die for me, I will not die for you.   690
You like the sunlight. Don't you think your father does?
I count the time I have to spend down there as long,
and the time to live is little, but that little is sweet.
You fought shamelessly for a way to escape death,
and passed your proper moment, and are still alive   695
because you killed her. Then, you wretch, you dare to call
me coward, when you let your woman outdare you,
and die for her magnificent young man? I see.
You have found a clever scheme by which you *never* will die.
You will always persuade the wife you have at the time   700
to die for you instead. And you, so low, then dare
blame your own people for not wanting to do this.
Silence. I tell you, as you cherish your own life,
all other people cherish theirs. And if you call
us names, you will be called names, and the names are true.   705

Chorus

Too much evil has been said in this speech and in
that spoken before. Old sir, stop cursing your own son.

Admetus

No, speak, and I will speak too. If it hurts to hear
the truth, you should not have made a mistake with me.

Pheres

I should have made a mistake if I had died for you.   710

Admetus

Is it the same thing to die old and to die young?

Pheres

Yes. We have only one life and not two to live.

Admetus

I think you would like to live a longer time than Zeus.

Pheres

Cursing your parents, when they have done nothing to you?

Admetus

Yes, for I found you much in love with a long life.   715

Pheres

Who is it you are burying? Did not someone die?

Admetus

And that she died, you foul wretch, proves your cowardice.

Pheres

You cannot say that we were involved in her death.

Admetus

Ah.
I hope that some day you will stand in need of me.   720

Pheres

Go on, and court more women, so they all can die.

Admetus

Your fault. You were not willing to.

Pheres

                              No, I was not.
It is a sweet thing, this God's sunshine, sweet to see.

Admetus

That is an abject spirit, not a man's.

Pheres

                               You shall
not mock an old man while you carry out your dead.

Admetus

You will die in evil memory, when you do die.   725

Pheres

I do not care what they say of me when I am dead.

Admetus

How old age loses all the sense of shame.

Pheres

                                   She was
not shameless, you found; she was only innocent.

Admetus

Get out of here now and let me bury my dead.

Pheres

I'll go. You murdered her, and you can bury her.   730
But you will have her brothers still to face. You'll pay,
for Acastus is no longer counted as a man
unless he sees you punished for his sister's blood.

Admetus

Go and be damned, you and that woman who lives with you.
Grow old as you deserve, childless, although your son   735
still lives. You shall not come again under the same roof
with me. And if I had to proclaim by heralds that I
disowned my father's house, I should have so proclaimed.

                                   (Pheres goes off.)
Now we, for we must bear the sorrow that is ours,
shall go, and lay her body on the burning place.   740

Chorus

Ah, cruel the price of your daring,

O generous one, O noble and brave,
farewell. May Hermes of the world below
and Hades welcome you. And if, even there,
the good fare best, may you have high honor   745
and sit by the bride of Hades.

(The body is borne off, followed by Admetus, servants, and Chorus.
Thus the stage is empty. Then enter, from the house, the
servant who was put in charge of Heracles.)

Servant

I have known all sorts of foreigners who have come in
from all over the world here to Admetus' house,
and I have served them dinner, but I never yet
have had a guest as bad as this to entertain.   750
In the first place, he could see the master was in mourning,
but inconsiderately came in anyway.
Then, he refused to understand the situation
and be content with anything we could provide,
but when we failed to bring him something, demanded it,   755
and took a cup with ivy on it in both hands
and drank the wine of our dark mother, straight, until
the flame of the wine went all through him, and heated him,
and then he wreathed branches of myrtle on his head
and howled, off key. There were two kinds of music now   760
to hear, for while he sang and never gave a thought
to the sorrows of Admetus, we servants were mourning
our mistress; but we could not show before our guest
with our eyes wet. Admetus had forbidden that.
So now I have to entertain this guest inside,   765
this ruffian thief, this highwayman, whatever he is,
while she is gone away from the house, and I could not
say goodbye, stretch my hand out to her in my grief
for a mistress who was like a mother to all the house
and me. She gentled her husband's rages, saved us all   770
from trouble after trouble. Am I not then right
to hate this guest who has come here in our miseries?

(Enter Heracles from the house, drunk, but not hopelessly so.)

Heracles

You there, with the sad and melancholy face, what is
the matter with you? The servant who looks after guests
should be polite and cheerful and not scowl at them.   775
But look at you. Here comes your master's dearest friend
to visit you, and you receive him with black looks
and frowns, all because of some trouble somewhere else.
Come here, I'll tell you something that will make you wise.
Do you really know what things are like, the way they are?   780
I don't think so. How could you? Well then, listen to me.
Death is an obligation which we all must pay.
There is not one man living who can truly say
if he will be alive or dead on the next day.
Fortune is dark; she moves, but we cannot see the way   785
nor can we pin her down by science and study her.
There, I have told you. Now you can understand. Go on,
enjoy yourself, drink, call the life you live today
your own, but only that, the rest belongs to chance.
Then, beyond all gods, pay your best attentions to   790
the Cyprian, man's sweetest. There's a god who's kind.
Let all this business go and do as I prescribe
for you, that is, if I seem to talk sense. Do I?
I think so. Well, then, get rid of this too-much grief,
put flowers on your head and drink with us, fight down   795
these present troubles; later, I know very well
that the wine splashing in the bowl will shake you loose
from these scowl-faced looks and the tension in your mind.
We are only human. Our thoughts should be human too,
since, for these solemn people and these people who scowl,   800
the whole parcel of them, if I am any judge,
life is not really life but a catastrophe.

Servant

I know all that. But we have troubles on our hands
now, that make revelry and laughter out of place.

Heracles

The dead woman is out of the family. Do not mourn   805
too hard. The master and the mistress are still alive.

Servant

What do you mean, alive? Do you not know what happened?

Heracles

Certainly, unless your master has lied to me.

Servant

He is too hospitable, too much.

Heracles

                         Should I not then
have enjoyed myself, because some outside woman was dead?   810

Servant

She was an outsider indeed. That is too true.

Heracles

Has something happened that he did not tell me about?

Servant

Never mind. Go. Our masters' sorrows are our own.

Heracles

These can be no outsiders' troubles.

Servant

                         If they were,
I should not have minded seeing you enjoy yourself.   815

Heracles

Have I been scandalously misled by my own friends?

Servant

You came here when we were not prepared to take in guests.
You see, we are in mourning. You can see our robes
of black, and how our hair is cut short.

Heracles

                       Who is dead?
The aged father? One of the children who is gone?   820

Servant

My lord, Admetus' wife is dead.

Heracles

What are you saying?
And all this time you were making me comfortable?

Servant

He could not bear to turn you from this house of his.

Heracles

My poor Admetus, what a helpmeet you have lost!

Servant

We are all dead and done for now, not only she.   825

Heracles

I really knew it when I saw the tears in his eyes,
his shorn hair and his face; but he persuaded me
with talk of burying someone who was not by blood
related. So, unwillingly, I came inside
and drank here in the house of this hospitable man   830
when he was in this trouble! Worse, I wreathed my head
with garlands, and drank freely. But you might have said
something about this great disaster in the house.
Now, where shall I find her? Where is the funeral being held?

Servant

Go straight along the Larisa road, and when you clear   835
the city you will see the monument and the mound.

(*He goes into the house, leaving Heracles alone on the stage.*)

Heracles

O heart of mine and hand of mine, who have endured
so much already, prove what kind of son it was
Alcmene, daughter of Electryon, bore to Zeus
in Tiryns. I must save this woman who has died   840
so lately, bring Alcestis back to live in this house,
and pay Admetus all the kindness that I owe.
I must go there and watch for Death of the black robes,
master of dead men, and I think I shall find him

drinking the blood of slaughtered beasts beside the grave.   845
Then, if I can break suddenly from my hiding place,
catch him, and hold him in the circle of these arms,
there is no way he will be able to break my hold
on his bruised ribs, until he gives the woman up
to me. But if I miss my quarry, if he does not come   850
to the clotted offering, I must go down, I must ask
the Maiden and the Master in the sunless homes
of those below; and I have confidence I shall bring
Alcestis back, and give her to the arms of my friend
who did not drive me off but took me into his house   855
and, though he staggered under the stroke of circumstance,
hid it, for he was noble and respected me.
Who in all Thessaly is a truer friend than this?
Who in all Greece? Therefore, he must not ever say
that, being noble, he befriended a worthless man.   860

(*He goes out. Presently Admetus comes on,*
followed by the Chorus.)

Admetus

Hateful is this
return, hateful the sight of this house
widowed, empty. Where shall I go?
Where shall I stay? What shall I say?
How can I die?
My mother bore me to a heavy fate.   865
I envy the dead. I long for those
who are gone, to live in their houses, with them.
There is no pleasure in the sunshine
nor the feel of the hard earth under my feet.
Such was the hostage Death has taken   870
from me, and given to Hades.

(*As they chant this, Admetus moans inarticulately.*)

Chorus

Go on, go on. Plunge in the deep of the house.
What you have suffered is enough for tears.
You have gone through pain, I know,

but you do no good to the woman who lies   875
below. Never again to look on the face
of the wife you loved hurts you.

Admetus

You have opened the wound torn in my heart.
What can be worse for a man than to lose
a faithful wife. I envy those   880
without wives, without children. I wish I had not
ever married her, lived with her in this house.
We have each one life. To grieve for this
is burden enough.
When we could live single all our days   885
without children, it is not to be endured
to see children sicken or married love
despoiled by death.

                                                    (As before.)
Chorus

Chance comes. It is hard to wrestle against it.
There is no limit to set on your pain.   890
The weight is heavy. Yet still
bear up. You are not the first man to lose
his wife. Disaster appears, to crush
one man now, but afterward another.

Admetus

How long my sorrows, the pain for my loves   895
down under the earth.
Why did you stop me from throwing myself
in the hollow cut of the grave, there to lie
dead beside her, who was best on earth?
Then Hades would have held fast two lives,   900
not one, and the truest of all, who crossed
the lake of the dead together.

Chorus

There was a man
of my people, who lost a boy

any house would mourn for,   905
the only child. But still
he carried it well enough,. though childless,
and he stricken with age
and the hair gray on him,
well on through his lifetime.   910

Admetus

O builded house, how shall I enter you?
How live, with this turn
of my fortune? How different now and then.
Then it was with Pelian pine torches,   915
with marriage songs, that I entered my house,
with the hand of a sweet bride on my arm,
with loud rout of revelers following
to bless her who now is dead, and me,
for our high birth, for nobilities   920
from either side which were joined in us.
Now the bridal chorus has changed for a dirge,
and for white robes the costumed black
goes with me inside
to where her room stands deserted.   925

Chorus

Your luck had been
good, so you were inexperienced when
grief came. Still you saved
your own life and substance.
Your wife is dead, your love forsaken.   930
What is new in this? Before
now death has parted
many from their wives.

Admetus

Friends, I believe my wife is happier than I   935
although I know she does not seem to be. For her,
there will be no more pain to touch her ever again.

She has her glory and is free from much distress.
But I, who should not be alive, who have passed by
my moment, shall lead a sorry life. I see it now.   940
How can I bear to go inside this house again?
Whom shall I speak to, who will speak to me, to give
me any pleasure in coming home? Where shall I turn?
The desolation in my house will drive me out
when I see my wife's bed empty, when I see the chairs   945
she used to sit in, and all about the house the floor
unwashed and dirty, while the children at my knees
huddle and cry for their mother and the servants mourn
their mistress and remember what the house has lost.
So it will be at home, but if I go outside   950
meeting my married friends in Thessaly, the sight
of their wives will drive me back, for I cannot endure
to look at my wife's agemates and the friends of her youth.
And anyone who hates me will say this of me:
"Look at the man, disgracefully alive, who dared   955
not die, but like a coward gave his wife instead
and so escaped death. Do you call him a man at all?
He turns on his own parents, but he would not die
himself." Besides my other troubles, they will speak
about me thus. What have I gained by living, friends,   960
when reputation, life, and action all are bad?

Chorus

I myself, in the transports
of mystic verses, as in study
of history and science, have found
nothing so strong as Compulsion,   965
nor any means to combat her,
not in the Thracian books set down
in verse by the school of Orpheus,
not in all the remedies Phoebus has given the heirs   970
of Asclepius to fight the many afflictions of man.

She alone is a goddess
without altar or image to pray

before. She heeds no sacrifice. 975
Majesty, bear no harder
on me than you have in my life before!
All Zeus even ordains
only with you is accomplished.
By strength you fold and crumple the steel of the Chalybes. 980
There is no pity in the sheer barrier of your will.

(*They turn and speak directly to Admetus, who
remains in the background.*)

Now she has caught your wife in the breakless grip of her hands.
Take it. You will never bring back, by crying, 985
the dead into the light again.
Even the sons of the gods fade
and go in death's shadow. 990
She was loved when she was with us.
She shall be loved still, now she is dead.
It was the best of all women to whom you were joined in
marriage.

The monument of your wife must not be counted among the
graves 995
of the dead, but it must be given its honors
as gods are, worship of wayfarers.
And as they turn the bend of the road 1000
and see it, men shall say:
"She died for the sake of her husband.
Now she is a blessed spirit.
Hail, majesty, be gracious to us." Thus will men speak in her
presence. 1005

But here is someone who looks like Alcmene's son,
Admetus. He seems on his way to visit you.

(*Heracles enters, leading a veiled woman by the hand.*)

Heracles

A man, Admetus, should be allowed to speak his mind
to a friend, instead of keeping his complaints suppressed
inside him. Now, I thought I had the right to stand 1010

beside you and endure what you endured, so prove
my friendship. But you never told me that she, who lay
dead, was your wife, but entertained me in your house
as if your mourning were for some outsider's death.
And so I wreathed my head and poured libations out   1015
to the gods, in your house, though your house had suffered so.
This was wrong, wrong I tell you, to have treated me
thus, though I have no wish to hurt you in your grief.
Now, as for the matter of why I have come back again,
I will tell you. Take this woman, keep her safe for me,   1020
until I have killed the master of the Bistones
and come back, bringing with me the horses of Thrace.
If I have bad luck—I hope not, I hope to come
back home—I give her to the service of your house.
It cost a struggle for her to come into my hands.   1025
You see, I came on people who were holding games
for all comers, with prizes which an athlete might
well spend an effort winning.

(Points to the woman.)
                      Here is the prize I won
and bring you. For the winners in the minor events
were given horses to take away, while those who won   1030
the heavier stuff, boxing and wrestling, got oxen,
and a woman was thrown in with them. Since I happened
to be there, it seemed wrong to let this splendid prize
go by. As I said, the woman is for you to keep.
She is not stolen. It cost me hard work to bring   1035
her here. Some day, perhaps, you will say I have done well.

Admetus

I did not mean to dishonor nor belittle you
when I concealed the fate of my unhappy wife,
but it would have added pain to pain already there
if you had been driven to shelter with some other host.   1040
This sorrow is mine. It is enough for me to weep.
As for the woman, if it can be done, my lord,

I beg you, have some other Thessalian, who has not
suffered as I have, keep her. You have many friends
in Pherae. Do not bring my sorrows back to me.   1045
I would not have strength to see her in my house and keep
my eyes dry. I am weak now. Do not add weakness
to my weakness. I have sorrow enough to weigh me down.
And where could a young woman live in this house? For
she is young, I can see it in her dress, her style.   1050
Am I to put her in the same quarters with the men?
And how, circulating among young men, shall she be kept
from harm? Not easy, Heracles, to hold in check
a young strong man. I am thinking of your interests.
Or shall I put her in my lost wife's chamber, keep   1055
her there? How can I take her to Alcestis' bed?
I fear blame from two quarters, from my countrymen
who might accuse me of betraying her who helped
me most, by running to the bed of another girl,
and from the dead herself. Her honor has its claim   1060
on me. I must be very careful. You, lady,
whoever you are, I tell you that you have the form
of my Alcestis; all your body is like hers.
Too much. Oh, for God's pity, take this woman away
out of my sight. I am beaten already, do not beat   1065
me again. For as I look on her, I think I see
my wife. It churns my heart to tumult, and the tears
break streaming from my eyes. How much must I endure
the bitter taste of sorrow which is still so fresh?

Chorus

I cannot put a good name to your fortune; yet   1070
whoever you are, you must endure what the god gives.

Heracles

I only wish that my strength had been great enough
for me to bring your wife back from the chambered deep
into the light. I would have done that grace for you.

Admetus

I know you would have wanted to. Why speak of it?   1075
There is no way for the dead to come back to the light.

Heracles

Then do not push your sorrow. Bear it as you must.

Admetus

Easier to comfort than to suffer and be strong.

Heracles

But if you wish to mourn for always, what will you gain?

Admetus

Nothing. I know it. But some impulse of my love   1080
makes me.

Heracles

        Why, surely. Love for the dead is cause for tears.

Admetus

Her death destroyed me, even more than I can say.

Heracles

You have lost a fine wife. Who will say you have not?

Admetus

                           So fine
that I, whom you see, never shall be happy again.

Heracles

Time will soften it. The evil still is young and strong.   1085

Admetus

You can say time will soften it, if time means death.

Heracles

A wife, love, your new marriage will put an end to this.

Admetus

Silence! I never thought you would say a thing like that.

Heracles

What? You will not remarry but keep an empty bed?

Admetus

No woman ever shall sleep in my arms again.   1090

Heracles

Do you believe you help the dead by doing this?

Admetus

Wherever she may be, she deserves my honors still.

Heracles

Praiseworthy, yes, praiseworthy. And yet foolish, too.

Admetus

Call me so, then, but never call me a bridegroom.

Heracles

I admire you for your faith and love you bear your wife.   1095

Admetus

Let me die if I betray her, though she is gone.

Heracles

                                        Well then,
receive this woman into your most generous house.

Admetus

Please, in the name of Zeus your father, no!

Heracles

                              And yet
you will be making a mistake if you do not;

Admetus

and eaten at the heart with anguish if I do.   1100

Heracles

Obey. The grace of this may come where you need grace.

Admetus

Ah.
I wish you had never won her in those games of yours.

Heracles

Where I am winner, you are winner along with me.

Admetus

Honorably said. But let the woman go away.

Heracles

She will go, if she should. First look. See if she should.   1105

Admetus

She should, unless it means you will be angry with me.

Heracles

Something I know of makes me so insistent with you.

Admetus

So, have your way. But what you do does not please me.

Heracles

The time will come when you will thank me. Only obey.

Admetus (*to attendants*)

Escort her in, if she must be taken into this house.   1110

Heracles

I will not hand this lady over to attendants.

Admetus

You yourself lead her into the house then, if you wish.

Heracles

I will put her into your hands and into yours alone.

Admetus

I will not touch her. But she is free to come inside.

Heracles

No, I have faith in your right hand, and only yours.   1115

Admetus

My lord, you are forcing me to act against my wish.

Heracles

Be brave. Reach out your hand and take the stranger's.

Admetus

So.

Here is my hand; I feel like Perseus killing the gorgon.

Heracles

You have her?

Admetus

        Yes, I have her.

Heracles

                Keep her, then. Some day
you will say the son of Zeus came as your generous guest.   1120
But look at her. See if she does not seem most like
your wife. Your grief is over now. Your luck is back.

Admetus

Gods, what shall I think! Amazement beyond hope, as I
look on this woman, this wife. Is she really mine,
or some sweet mockery for God to stun me with?   1125

Heracles

Not so. This is your own wife you see. She is here.

Admetus

Be careful she is not some phantom from the depths.

Heracles

The guest and friend you took was no necromancer.

Admetus

Do I see my wife, whom I was laying in the grave?

Heracles

Surely. But I do not wonder at your unbelief.   1130

Admetus

May I touch her, and speak to her, as my living wife?

Heracles

Speak to her. All that you desired is yours.

Admetus

                    Oh, eyes
and body of my dearest wife, I have you now
beyond all hope. I never thought to see you again.

Heracles

You have her. May no god hate you for your happiness.   1135

Admetus

O nobly sprung child of all-highest Zeus, may good
fortune go with you. May the father who gave you birth
keep you. You alone raised me up when I was down.
How did you bring her back from down there to the light?

Heracles

I fought a certain deity who had charge of her.   1140

Admetus

Where do you say you fought this match with Death?

Heracles

Beside
the tomb itself. I sprang and caught him in my hands.

Admetus

But why is my wife standing here, and does not speak?

Heracles

You are not allowed to hear her speak to you until
her obligations to the gods who live below   1145
are washed away. Until the third morning comes. So now
take her and lead her inside, and for the rest of time,
Admetus, be just. Treat your guests as they deserve.
and now goodbye. I have my work that I must do,
and go to face the lordly son of Sthenelus.   1150

Admetus

No, stay with us and be the guest of our hearth.

Heracles

There still
will be a time for that, but I must press on now.

Admetus

Success go with you. May you find your way back here.

(*Heracles goes.*)

I proclaim to all the people of my tetrarchy
that, for these blessed happenings, they shall set up
dances, and the altars smoke with sacrifice offered.   1155

For now we shall make our life again, and it will be
a better one.

     I was lucky. That I cannot deny.

        (He takes Alcestis by the hand and leads
          her inside the house.)

Chorus (going)

  Many are the forms of what is unknown.
  Much that the gods achieve is surprise.   1160
  What we look for does not come to pass;
  God finds a way for what none foresaw.
  Such was the end of this story.